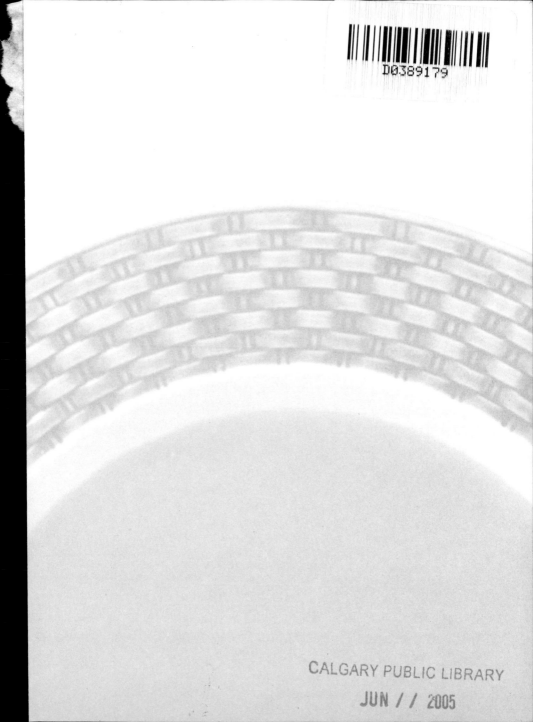

D0389179

THE
UNEMPLOYMENT
SURVIVAL
GUIDE

THE UNEMPLOYMENT SURVIVAL GUIDE

Jim Stringham and David R. Workman

Gibbs Smith, Publisher
Salt Lake City

First Edition
08 07 06 05 04   5 4 3 2 1

Published by
Gibbs Smith, Publisher
P.O. Box 667
Layton, Utah 84041

Orders: (1-800) 748-5439
www.gibbs-smith.com

Cover design by Kurt Wahlner
Designed and produced by Gotham Design, NYC
Printed and bound in Hong Kong

Library of Congress Cataloging-in-Publication Data
Stringham, Jim.
The unemployment survival guide / Jim Stringham, and David R.
Workman.—1st ed.
    p. cm.
 ISBN 1-58685-373-2
 1. Unemployment—Psychological aspects. 2. Unemployed—Psychology.
I. Workman, David R. II. Title.
HD5708 .S76 2004
650.1—dc22
                        2003024949

CONTENTS

PREFACE

Unemployment can be one of the most stressful periods of your life. We know because we've both been there. We've lived in the trenches. We know what you're going through and it isn't easy. Millions of people each year are unemployed. Their unemployment experience may also affect others who care about them and their well-being. Trust us, these people are not saying this is one of the happiest times of their lives.

The first night we worked on this book, Jim was in his eighth year of counseling people facing this issue, and David was facing his first day of unemployment after three years with the Salt Lake Olympic Committee. Inspiration flowed easily between us. After writing collaboratively for a week, we immediately saw the value as we dealt with issues like the sense of isolation, resentment, loss of humor and daily joy, stressed personal relationships, and feeling more comfortable with a lower standard of living.

Our aspiration is to begin a dialogue that addresses and raises awareness of the emotional difficulties brought on by unemployment. Hopefully, this guide will help you add a little joy, happiness, and fun to your life during this difficult and unsettling time.

> *— The Authors*

ACKNOWLEDGMENTS

Paula Callister,
the unsung hero.

Janet Yowell,
contributing editor extraordinaire.

INTRODUCTION

This book will help make life more bearable while searching for employment. It won't teach you how to find a job, but it will teach you how to keep from going crazy if you're between jobs, living paycheck to paycheck, worrying about losing your job, or if you have recently retired. This information has been tested and proven beneficial for a wide variety of people—from laid-off, highly paid executives to individuals just entering or reentering the workforce. Certainly, part of finding a new job is preparing and sending résumés, perusing classified ads, searching for employment on the Internet, networking, and interviewing. But until you find work—and you will find work—your biggest, most-important job is taking care of you. Hopefully, you'll never have the need to read this book, but in case you do—and most likely you or someone you love will—it should serve as a guide to improving your daily life while you're unemployed.

For the purposes of this discussion, unemployed means you're jobless, looking for a job, and available for work. At some point in your life, you, your partner, a parent, a friend, or a neighbor will find yourselves between jobs or out of work. Keep in mind that more than 95 percent of the population seeking employment was terminated from previous positions for reasons other than job performance. Over the past twelve years, the unemployment rate in the United States has ranged between 3.9 and 7.8 percent. If we placed a population value on this number, consider this: At the printing of this book, a 6.4 percent rate equates approximately 9.4 million people. This statistic, while grim, does not include the estimated 4.8 million people working part-time who want full-time jobs and another 1.4 million who have looked for work in the past year but not the last month, who are no longer counted by the U.S. Department of Labor as being unemployed. If unemployment were a disease, it would be deemed an epidemic. Looking for a job or seeking more successful employment isn't uncommon, nor is it embarrassing. Most importantly, you're not alone.

Finding a job is something we usually do alone and, in fact, can be socially difficult. It's often hard to find social support, unlike other challenges for which support groups such as Alcoholics Anonymous and Weight Watchers exist. Unemployment may be a bit less intriguing or mysterious to discuss in social circles since talk of one's emotional well-being while job hunting isn't usually of concern—unless you yourself are unemployed. There is an abundance of resources available on how to get a job, write a résumé, and even how to interview more effectively, but there isn't nearly enough information available on how to take care of you while unemployed. Don't be shocked to find that you may face many pressures and fears during your difficult—even discouraging—search for employment, but do know that you are not alone and resources do exist to help you get through the next few weeks, months, or longer periods of time if necessary. This sounds cheesy, but it's important: No matter how dreary a day you're having, remember that every rainbow is made from the proper balance of rain and sunshine. This book will help you in nurturing yourself while you discover what the next step is for you.

CHAPTER 1

REMEMBER, THIS TOO SHALL PASS

First and foremost, remember that you won't be unemployed forever! Unemployment seems to last forever, when in fact, it won't. Statistically, life looks good for you. You will find a job. On the average, it takes anywhere between three weeks and six months to find work. If you're looking for a minimum-wage job, it should take no longer than three weeks to find suitable employment. However, for a white-collar, higher-paying job, it may take three to six months in a healthy economy, but could be twelve to eighteen months or more in a sluggish or recessed economy. Regardless, many people don't find comfort in this statistic. To them, it feels like employment is never going to happen—that they'll be unemployed forever. No doubt about it, the days you're without a job are longer and time does slow down. The good news is, these days won't last forever; you will work again!

FACING BLACK MONDAY

Even though it may appear as though it is, the loss of your job isn't the end of the world. Your life isn't pointless or pathetic. On the other hand, the day after losing your job—the first day of your unemployment—may rank right up there with one of the worst days of your life. Typically, there's not one good thing about this day. This is the day (or maybe the week) to be a bum.

Stay up late. Go on, it's okay. You can sleep late in the morning. There's no need to shower, shave, or brush your teeth. Why even get dressed? Stay in your bathrobe all day. Eat an entire box of your favorite cereal. Better yet, eat an entire pint of ice cream. Order the biggest, cheesiest pizza and have it delivered right to your door. Let the dishes pile up in the sink and grow mold. Watch every trashy talk show and soap opera that daytime television can produce. Your first day home is very much like staying home sick from school (only better because you can order real food and watch anything you want on TV). You can even put a sign on your door that reads, "Happy-People-Not-Welcome Zone."

On Black Monday, don't rush into anything. You don't need to figure out what you're going to do with the rest of your life. Really, take a nap all afternoon; in fact, schedule the nap into your day! As the famous Scottish ballad proclaims, "I am hurt, but I am not slain. I [will] lay me down and bleed awhile, and then I [will] rise and fight again." You, too, will pull yourself up by your bootstraps and fight again, just not on Black Monday.

ACCEPT BEING UNEMPLOYED AS A FULL-TIME JOB

Ever wonder why you feel so tired when you're unemployed? The reason is because being unemployed is a difficult, full-time job in itself. It's demanding both physically and emotionally. As a matter of fact, it is a huge energy drain. Almost anyone who has been out of work will tell you there are few things worse on the mind, body, and soul than looking for work. Pressures relating to cash (or lack thereof), résumé writing, interviewing, networking, and job searching are some of the toughest challenges we might face. Job coaches report that even people who are unhappily employed avoid changing jobs because the search for employment can be so difficult and emotionally draining.

Finding a new job can be a wonderful challenge or adversity to overcome. It can be a great business. Why? It can be an opportunity for growth and experience. It requires you to be on top of your game. Many people discover that finding new work is actually one of the most challenging jobs there is. It will utilize a full range of skills:

- **Creativity:** You will use creativity in everything you do, from managing your finances and finding the right job to discovering joy in your life.

- **Patience:** A hefty dose of patience with yourself, others, and potential employers will get you through the long process of finding your next meaningful job.

- **Perseverance:** Stay on top of leads for open jobs and keep networking to increase your chances for meeting a person who can help in your search. Keep checking in with staffing companies, classifieds, and Internet job searches, and be sure to make follow-up phone calls to companies you have already interviewed with.

- **Humor and fun:** Keeping a sense of humor will help you maintain a positive disposition. Try not to take yourself too seriously. It's a good idea to plan on doing something fun after a day of job-searching: meet a friend for a latte at a coffeehouse, go to an ice cream shop for a triple-dipped ice cream cone, go out to your favorite club for a night of dancing, see a funny movie, have a water fight with your kids or take them to the zoo. Allow yourself to be silly. These things will keep you active and relieve some of the heavy burden you may be feeling to find another job.

- **Assertiveness:** Go after the opportunities you want most and work to create your new future. If you have landed an interview with the company of your dreams, then speak up and tell them why you are the one for the job!

- **Kindness:** Most people are very hard on themselves during this process. Being kind to yourself has its practical applications. If you are kind to yourself it will project to others. Treat yourself and others well and life will be good to you in return. Remember that kindness can go a long way in opening doors that may otherwise be closed to you. Send a thank-you card to companies that took the time to interview you or to someone who has opened the door for you to get an interview. Make time each day to do something nice just for yourself.

- Intelligence: Working smartly while trying to find a job is a science unto itself. Know how to send résumés that will actually get the attention you deserve. If you're not doing it properly, you can send 500 résumés and not get one response. No matter what the job, once you are invited for an interview, do your homework and research the company you are visiting beforehand. Become a master in the art of interviewing. There is a reason why an interview is weighted so heavily in the hiring process. At this stage, the person who presents himself or herself the most effectively will likely get the job.

If gaining experience and overcoming challenges and adversity are important to you, unemployment might just be the best full-time job out there. When asked, you don't have to tell people you've been laid off or you're between jobs; instead, you can tell them you're working full time on finding your next job.

Dealing with Your Loss

People tend to believe that the experience and feelings of grief and loss are only associated with the death of a family member or friend. However, emotions associated with grief and loss may vary with intensity and stem from a variety of events such as health failure, accidents, burglary of your home or car, death of a pet, or your close friend moving away. You should expect to go through the normal grieving emotions related to loss:

- Shock: Being unprepared for such a dramatic change in your life.
- Denial: Not accepting or understanding what has happened to you at this moment of your life.

- **Sadness:** Coping with the disappointment over loss of identity, daily structure, loss of income, and sense of community.

- **Guilt:** Feeling responsible for what has happened.

- **Anger:** Experiencing disappointment in yourself and others for your current situation.

- **Acceptance:** Finding a sense of peace for your current station in life and making yourself available for future opportunities.

Clearly, losing a job is a significant loss in your life, probably on many fronts—cash flow, daily structure, working friends, family provider role, and even partly, your identity. Indeed, you'll experience all of the emotions that are associated with grief and loss. It helps to know that you'll eventually feel better with time—Mother Nature takes good care of us in this regard. The process of grief and loss is often tricky: People tend to think that it occurs step by step and that they'll experience these emotions in sequential order, similar to four quarters of a football game or nine innings of a baseball game. But, the process doesn't occur that way. You don't wake up one morning and say, "And now, it's time for the seventh inning sadness stretch!" Initially, you'll feel like you're almost entirely in shock, but gradually you'll progress through each of the emotions until a general acceptance is reached after a period of (possibly lengthy) time.

People often ask how much time is too much. When should professional advice be sought? There is no rule and everyone is different. As a guideline, when your everyday strategies for elevating your mood and decreasing stress are not working, no matter how short the time has been, you may want to consider talking to a professional. Most mental health professionals suggest seeking help after two months of not "pulling out." It is very common to seek therapy for relief of symptoms right away. There is no need to wait. There are several places that offer assistance in locating a therapist that will be right for you:

- Ask friends or family of anyone they know or like

- Look in the local Yellow Pages

- Community centers

- Check referral lists of local colleges and universities

- Consult your family doctor or other medical professionals for recommendations

Normal symptoms of grief and loss almost parallel symptoms of depression, but grief and loss don't constitute actual depression. The symptoms of both may include disturbed sleep, poor appetite, weight loss, isolation, and feelings of helplessness. Again, the length of time you experience them may constitute depression. Fortunately, counseling, medication, or environmental changes will help in any of these cases.

DISCARD RESENTMENT

Although it's common and normal to feel resentment toward someone else or even yourself after losing a job, it has a high price tag. Resentment is an emotion capable of destroying your happiness and your soul. When you remember an injustice, whether real or perceived, you are immediately flooded with stress hormones that take a heavy mental, emotional, and physical toll on your body. Over time, high levels of such hormones can actually lead to severe skin conditions, ulcers, strokes, and even heart attacks. The worst effect from experiencing resentment toward a former boss, colleague, company, or other institution is that you have needlessly burned up creativity and energy—two things you cannot afford to be without at this point in your life. To fully embrace the new beginning, it often helps to bring a certain semblance of closure to your previous situation. No matter whether you quit or were fired or laid off, you should consider doing things to make your transition smoother. Consider thanking your old boss or employer for the opportunity to work there. This can help free yourself from feelings of resentment, disappointment, and anger to support emotional availability for your next employer.

Also, it's common to sometimes feel resentment toward your general station in life, or toward others who appear to be succeeding financially or who are gainfully employed. The most destructive thing you can do, however, is to turn your anger and resentment toward yourself, which constitutes a kind of mental suicide. Look at your current status as an opportunity to learn about—and become better at—forgiving and letting go of resentment. Begin to free yourself from the poison of resentment by visiting these resources:

- *Alcoholics Anonymous Big Book*'s section on forgiveness

- *How to Forgive: 10 Guidelines* by Victor M. Parachin

- Forgiveness Works: **www.forgivenessworks.org**

People often confuse forgiveness with forgetting, excusing, condoning, reconciling, or weakness. Forgiveness is none of these. It is simply letting go of the resentment and taking charge of your own happiness rather than giving it away and letting somebody else decide for you. Forgiveness can be hard to do (you already know why). Besides the physical assault on your body, the emotional price tag is perhaps even greater. Lack of forgiveness causes many negative side effects:

- Gives others power over you

- Punishes you and nobody else

- Keeps you in the role of judge—a very destructive emotional coping strategy

- Teaches others, especially your children, by poor example

- Keeps you in the past rather than focused on the here and now or on your dreams for the future

If you struggle with forgiving, try a few of the following suggestions:

• Try to keep an open mind on forgiving others who you don't want to forgive.

• Forgive instantly rather than thinking about an event all day, month, or year.

• Cleanse yourself by reviewing your day and forgive anyone who has hurt you.

• Choose to be happy rather than right.

• Write a letter to the person who hurt you, but don't mail it. Bury it, burn it, or file it away.

• Listen to stories where people choose to forgive rather than hate.

• Remind yourself that by forgiving you are giving great gifts to yourself such as love, kindness, hope, contentment, and better health.

Remember that your time of unemployment is only temporary. When the time comes to work again, you will have acquired important skills to be used for the remainder of your life. As Eleanor Roosevelt said, "Yesterday is history, tomorrow is a mystery, but today is a gift." Enjoy your gift of life; do not waste energy getting caught up in resentment that leads nowhere.

PUT POVERTY IN PERSPECTIVE

You may feel poor during your time of unemployment, and your financial situation has likely changed temporarily for the worse, but bear in mind that the most dire economic situation for our country's citizens would be a welcome change for millions of people living just a short plane ride away. Views on worldwide poverty largely depend on perspective and your own economic reality. When losing their jobs, people are typically concerned with their own situation and less likely to think of someone else's plight halfway around the world or even down the street. This is said not to diminish the tremendous needs in the United States, but perhaps to offer a small amount of comfort and perspective to you during unemployment with this realization.

Many things we take for granted daily, such as proper health and basic nutrition, are serious global problems. Think about the following statistics and questions:

- According to UNICEF, each day in the developing world, 30,500 children die from preventable diseases such as diarrhea, acute respiratory infections, or malaria; malnutrition is associated with more than half of those deaths. That figure depicts the population of an average-size midwestern U.S. town.

- Do you have a non-dirt floor where you live? If so, then you are among the upper half of the world's richest people.

- Do you have a window, a door, and more than one room? You belong in the upper 20 percent of the world's richest people if you do.

- Can you read this book and do you have a pair of shoes, a change of underwear, and a choice from two or more foods to eat for your next meal? If your answer is yes, then you belong in the top 10 percent of the world's wealthiest.

- Do you have some sort of refrigeration? You are among the world's top 5 percent.

- Does your family have a car, a computer, a microwave, a refrigerator, and a VCR? You are among the 99th percentile of the most-wealthy people the world has ever known throughout its entire history if this is true for you. Unemployed or not, you are the elite, the top echelon of wealth and prosperity!

Virtually all of the American "poor" (as defined above) have access to a refrigerator, stove, oven, toilet, bathroom, toaster, electricity, phone, plumbing, transportation, and a host of other things that are considered absolute luxuries in other countries.

In stating this we don't mean to diminish your financial worries or emotional, physical, or spiritual struggles, but to offer you a more holistic, global perspective of your situation as it relates to the rest of the people on the planet.

Life is better than it seems at the moment.

Embrace the Uncertainty of Change

Is losing your job the end of the road or the beginning of the next one? This is similar to asking your view on whether the glass is half empty or half full. In either case, you want to make sure the glass gets to be full again. Many of us don't welcome change because we enjoy our comfort zones. But when change is thrust upon us, it can be rewarding to take full advantage of the situation.

To help begin your transition, start by asking for an exit interview from the company you are leaving. It will be helpful to go over some of your strong and weak points with your former employer, and to use their suggestions toward future job opportunities. If you were laid off due to company financial difficulties, perhaps you could ask about leads for other jobs in your field. Your former boss may have connections within the industry and may be able to assist you in networking. Also, ask if the company uses any particular staffing companies to help them fill open jobs. This will give you an idea of which staffing companies specialize in your industry and which ones will be the most beneficial to you while you're looking for your next job.

When you lose your job you tend to think so much has ended or died. Rather than a stumbling block, it can be a new adventure and an opportunity for growth, a steppingstone to what we need in life. Change is hard in any transition phase. When in a transitional phase, we tend to believe that all will be well when we have new jobs, new friends, a new lover, a new car, etc. Actually, much is well now. Every explorer dared to follow a dream where others lacked the courage to follow. So go exploring. This can be a good time to investigate new careers and a chance to rediscover yourself. Follow your passion if you so desire. If you have skills in another field of interest, develop a résumé and send it out as well as looking for jobs similar to the one you left behind. Taking a new job in a new field will most likely mean an entry-level position, lower pay, and not very good hours. But if this is the choice you make, and you're committed to it, the reward comes in doing something you love and being paid to do it—no matter how great or small the compensation may be. During this period of transition, you have the opportunity of taking a moment to reflect on your past jobs and other options so you can better evaluate what type of job to look for in the future and the right place to find it.

1. Describe your preferred working atmosphere. Is it a busy and high-paced environment? Or is it a quiet and serene atmosphere?

2. Do you like to work with people and on teams or more independently?

3. Do you prefer working with numbers, writing reports, or using your hands?

4. Do you prefer working in a job that gets you out of the office or is located inside?

5. Do you prefer high-profile, high-responsibility jobs or positions that are more behind the scenes?

6. Do you enjoy a more casual or formal working environment?

7. Do you have a long commute? Would you be willing to take a job for less pay that has a shorter commute? What do you do to make your commute more enjoyable?

8. Do you enjoy where you live or would you prefer to live someplace else?

9. What do you want to be when you grow up?

Life is a journey, a path, a road, and an ever-changing experience. This may also be an opportunity to move to a new location, a new city, a new state, or across the country. If you're looking for a new job, why not look in a place you would prefer to live. There's no reward if risks are never taken.

For those of you who can't wait to get back to your regular daily grind, the transition to a new job is also filled with opportunities and challenges. On one hand, you'll be leaving behind an office or workplace filled with friends and memories. On the other hand, it's a new beginning, a chance to do things right or better, and a time to meet new people and make new friends. Life itself is unique because you never know what the next day will bring. The state of happiness isn't a destination to reach, but the means by which you choose to travel. In times of transition, it's best to keep your spirits high and your outlook bright for the next adventure.

CHAPTER 2

BE GRATEFUL, GIVE THANKS

Sometimes it's easy to ignore or discount the wonderful blessings that surround us. We tend to focus more on what we feel is wrong rather than on what is right, or on what we don't have rather than on what we do. Right here, right now, start counting your blessings. One of the best coping strategies for handling difficult times is to take at least five minutes a day to count your blessings and be grateful for what you have. Notice the easy ones first:

- You got a good night's sleep and have a roof over your head.

- Your electricity works and you've got hot water on tap.

- You're spending time with your children, even for a moment.

- Your refrigerator is stocked relatively full and there's food on the table.

- You're not sick today.

- Your car is dependable and not in the shop.

- You can walk in your neighborhood without fear.

- You have family and friends who care for you or live close to you.

- You have a lot of colleagues and friends in your field.

- You have a high school, college, or graduate degree.

- Your spouse or friends (or even your dog, cat, bird, or fish) are there for you at the end of a hard day.

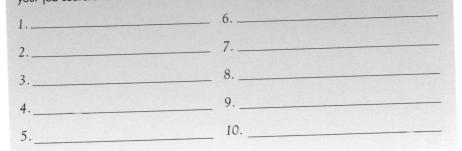

MOST THANKFUL FOR... Appreciate everything—from time with your friends to the freedoms we enjoy in this country. There are still billions of people on the planet who will never know the freedoms and opportunities you have. Celebrating the spirit of Thanksgiving on a daily basis will support you well throughout your job search. Take a moment and write down ten things that you're most thankful for:

1. _____   6. _____

2. _____   7. _____

3. _____   8. _____

4. _____   9. _____

5. _____   10. _____

LOOK FOR INSPIRATION

Sometimes we need inspirational images and stories to give us guidance and hope when we face our own trials. You can find inspiration in national headlines or find inspiration close to home in your own neighborhood:

- In 2001, a blind man climbed 29,000 feet to the summit of Mount Everest.

- In 2003, a cancer survivor won the Tour de France for the fifth year in a row.

- Nelson Mandela spent 27 years in a prison cell for challenging apartheid. While in prison, he could have one visitor per year for 30 minutes, and write and receive 1 letter every 6 months. After his release, he became the president of South Africa.

- Notice local heroes in your city's communities that help change or improve neighborhoods by reporting suspicious activity, keeping police informed of known drug houses in the area, or working to keep kids out of gangs and busy with community activities and clubs. Try to become active yourself by joining the neighborhood watch group or local community center.

- Look at your mother or father for inspiration. Did they raise you alone? Did they raise a large family successfully? Did your grandparents immigrate to another country and have to make a living from scratch? Be appreciative of the sacrifices they made to give you a better life.

- Visit your local children's hospital or a center for the physically challenged, and spend time with the residents. Get to know them. See the courage in their eyes.

MOST INSPIRING TO ME... However you do it, incorporate being inspired into your daily routine to assist you in reaching your goals and overcoming this period of uncertainty in your life. Finding inspiration is an individual process. What are the stories that inspire you? Take a moment to list events that have brought you inspiration.

_____

_____

_____

_____

If a blind man can climb to the top of Mt. Everest, then what's stopping you from reaching your goals? No hurdle is too high to jump, no problem too great to overcome, and no achievement beyond your reach.

FEED YOUR SOUL

When you are unemployed, you tend to look at the here and now. What activities give you the opportunity to look at the big picture of your life?

Having a spiritual component in your life is important to many people, regardless of circumstances, but when things are rough, you can feel the benefits even more. Here are some suggestions:

- Go camping and enjoy nature
- Do good deeds
- Meditate
- Practice yoga
- Attend concerts
- Read good books
- Keep a personal journal
- Compile your favorite inspirational quotes or post them on the fridge
- Look up your favorite passages from your favorite books. Look at what the authors have to say on happiness, peace, fear, endurance, compassion, and even humor
- Take a hot bath and light some candles
- Enjoy gardening
- Go for a walk and take in the beautiful surroundings

Spiritual beliefs and practices are quite personal and vary from person to person. But they all blend into a cohesive spiritual path that can raise your focus from the challenges immediately before you, help you find peace within the storm, and provide you with opportunities to help others. Spiritual beliefs and practices help you interact with a variety of people and provide a mechanism of support and guidance.

CHAPTER 3

BROADEN YOUR IDENTITY

Introductions between people frequently include the question "What do you do?" Look your new acquaintance straight in the eye and say, "I eat, I sleep, I get dressed . . . Oh . . . you mean for a living?" Too often, we use our job to define ourselves, when in reality what we do isn't who we are. Our jobs are an important characteristic of our profiles, but only part of the picture—no more, no less. One could argue that if you believe your job is your total identity, then chances are you were already unhappy before you were unemployed. We all can recognize that our character and actions are the primary fabric of who we are that define us—not our cars, our houses, or our level of income. Each of us has many possible identities:

- Parent
- Athlete
- Teacher
- Counselor

- Spouse
- Mentor
- Humanitarian
- Provider

- Sibling
- Student
- Volunteer

Perhaps some of these identities listed above describe you. Which ones would you like to maintain, add, or delete in your life?

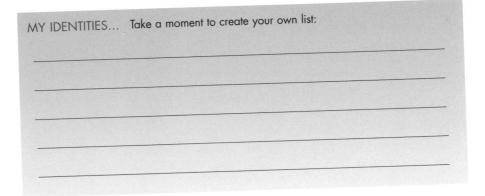

MY IDENTITIES... Take a moment to create your own list:

True, a job is part of the picture that defines us, and it's important, but it's just one part of the personal puzzle that makes us who we are. We can define our lives in so many different ways, often based on family, friends, skills and talents, knowledge, personal experiences, hobbies, spiritual development, even pets. The answer to "who we are" or "what we do" isn't as simple as saying, "I'm in sales."

MAINTAIN A DAILY STRUCTURE

Now that you've let your hair grow, eaten junk food, skipped bathing, let the dishes stack up, and worn the same clothes for a week, it's time to add some structure back into your life. You'll know when the time is right to begin this process. And, if you don't know—trust us—your friends will warn you with shrewd hints such as, "You know, Dirty Dishes is not an air freshener scent sold in stores."

Being employed gives you a sense of purpose and a place to go every day (even if you hate your job and boss). Now is the time to rededicate yourself and find a sense of purpose. Feel free to reestablish your old routine. If you got up at 6 a.m., then start getting up at 6 a.m. again. If you went to bed at

10 p.m., then go to bed at 10 p.m. again. Don't stay up all night watching TV, and don't sleep in until noon. You want your day to get back to how it used to be, but instead of working your job, you'll be working on getting your next job. Your day should be the same, your habits and routine the same, but now you spend 9 to 5 looking for a new job.

Take a moment to fill in the appropriate times during the day to keep an active schedule. If something doesn't fit, rearrange the schedule until it does, and be sure to give yourself plenty of time to get everything done during the day.

MY SCHEDULE...

Get Up:	Work:
Have Breakfast:	Run Any Errands:
Get Ready:	End of the Day:
Work:	Work Out:
Break:	Return Home:
Work:	Dinner Time:
Lunch Time:	Household Chores:
Work:	Relax, Family Time:
Break:	Go to Bed:

The first step is to follow your normal morning ritual—eat breakfast, drink coffee and juice, and read your favorite sections of the paper—but look at the classifieds last. Then follow this with a morning of dedicated hard work comprised of all the tasks necessary to find a job. Schedule a lunch break, follow that with an afternoon of work, and end the day at 5 p.m. Be sure to take appropriate breaks throughout the day—in fact, schedule a couple of extra ones just to keep your head clear.

Maintain a good appearance: Shave, bathe, wash and cut or style your hair, dress nicely, and keep your car and house well maintained. If you keep a positive outlook and a routine, success will follow. Remember to dress for success—you never know when you'll need to look your best for interviews that are scheduled with short notice or meet somebody who may open a door for you. The bottom line is, the more normal your professional daily routine, the more confident you will feel about tackling the task of finding your next job.

GET YOUR BEAUTY REST

Sleep. Get your rest. After that first adjustment period, don't stay up all night because you can. Just like when you were a kid, make every night during the week a school night. You can't expect to perform well the next day if you don't get adequate rest. You need six to eight hours of sleep each night. If you're not sleeping well, investigate your nighttime routine:

- Is your room too light?

- Are you eating full meals close to the time you retire in the evening?

- Are you drinking coffee or caffeinated sodas late at night?

- Do you have any medical conditions causing pain?

- Is your bedroom temperature uncomfortable?

- Are you exercising too late in the evening or not at all?

- Are you drinking too much alcohol?

- Do you smoke before bedtime?

- Are you using recreational drugs?

- Have you taken a hot shower or bath before bedtime to help you relax?

If you were sleeping well before you lost your job and you're not now, it's probably just a short-term, stress-related problem. If your sleep is agitated or continues for a prolonged period of time, it may be a symptom of depression.

When under stress, sleep patterns often change. You may oversleep as a form of withdrawal, not wanting to deal with everyday life; it's just a common symptom of being down. If it persists for an extended period of time, consult your physician for the appropriate treatment or visit a therapist to talk about what's keeping you awake at night. If you're having difficulty falling asleep, try some of these well-known suggestions on how to get a better night's rest:

- Establish a regular schedule for your day and stick to it. When it's time for bed, it's time for bed. Create a routine that begins to relax you as much as one hour before bedtime each day. Read a book, take a warm bath or hot shower, or listen to relaxing nature tapes with sounds of the forest, ocean, or calming rhythmic tones.

- Avoid stimulants in the evening hours. These include caffeinated drinks, chocolate, and nicotine. They will revive you and keep you from sleeping. In addition to the stimulants, you may also want to limit or reduce the amount of alcohol you consume prior to bedtime. Although it's a depressant, alcohol will actually disturb your sleep during the night.

- On the flip side, try a cup of noncaffeinated herbal tea: anise, catnip, chamomile, or fennel.

- Avoid taking naps late in the afternoon or early evening.

- The primary purpose for the bedroom is sleeping. For a good night's rest try associating the bedroom with sleeping activities. A laptop or the TV may stimulate your senses instead of relaxing them.

- If you are not getting enough sleep, don't worry over it. That will only make matters worse. Some people wake up in the middle of the night, look at the clock, and begin to worry over how many hours they have left to sleep before they actually have to get up. If this is a problem, move the clock to a place where you won't look at it.

- If you can't fall asleep within half an hour after going to bed, get out of bed and engage in a relaxing activity until you're sleepy.

- Eat a healthy dinner a few hours before bedtime. Eat foods rich in the amino acid L-tryptophan: warm milk, walnuts, cashews, chicken, cottage cheese, sunflower seeds, bananas, or turkey. L-tryptophan is used by the brain to produce serotonin, which helps to induce sleep. If needed, have a light snack before bedtime.

You can also receive helpful tips and information about sleeping from these Web sites:

- The National Sleep Foundation: **www.sleepfoundation.org**

- American Academy of Sleep Medicine: **www.aasmnet.org**

- Sleepnet.com: **www.sleepnet.com**

Sleeping well is necessary for your emotional well-being. A well-rested body equals a clear mind. Without sleep, it is hard to function at your best. And, like never before, you need to function well while you search for your next job.

- Avoid exercising at least three or four hours before bedtime. Exercise increases your heart rate and raises your body temperature—two things that will keep you awake.

- Make sure your bedroom and your bed are comfortable. Keep the temperature cool and make sure your mattress is the way you like it. Be sure to keep your room dark and, if necessary, use a fan as a white-noise generator or ear plugs to block out unwanted sounds.

RUN FOR YOUR LIFE

If there's a magic pill for mental and physical health, exercise is it. The most effective (and often least expensive) type of exercise is anything cardiovascular; it improves circulation, burns calories, reduces risk of heart disease, lowers stress levels, increases endurance, lowers blood pressure, and prevents diabetes. It's important to maintain a healthy lifestyle under any circumstances, but you'll never feel exercise making more of a difference in your life than now. Trust us on this: Exercise is a good thing. You'll think and feel better about yourself. In fact, under difficult situations, exercise is imperative and does not have to be expensive. Community centers, public parks, and schools have indoor and outdoor facilities. Do some of these activities to increase your heart rate:

- Power walking
- Hiking
- Rowing
- Cross-country skiing
- Rope jumping
- Tai Chi
- Running
- Swimming
- Stair climbing
- Basketball
- Yoga
- Mountain climbing
- Cycling
- Pumping iron
- Aerobics
- Frisbee
- Dancing
- Clean the house or yard vigorously

You should plan to do a cardiovascular activity thirty minutes or longer, three or four days a week. If you are also trying to lose weight, you can increase the time to five or six days a week. It's also a good idea to know what your resting heart rate is and monitor your heart rate after a cardio-vascular workout. This will tell you how beneficial your effort is during exercise. Before beginning any new exercise regime, it is always best to consult a physician. Here are some advantages to exercising:

- Stimulates the immune system, which reduces illness
- Raises self-confidence
- Reduces fatigue and helps us to sleep better
- Lowers the risk of high cholesterol, heart disease, heart attacks, high blood pressure, and some cancers
- Aids in keeping lean muscle, which deteriorates with age
- Reduces stress

Recognize that exercise is an important habit to include in your daily activities. Find your own schedule, the best time of the day, and the best exercises. Run for your life!

EAT TO LIVE, DON'T LIVE TO EAT

Eat right. It will affect your mood. Food will either give you energy or make you groggy. According to the United States Surgeon General, more than half of all Americans struggle with being overweight. Often, we have heard a friend or family member say, "I gained 10 pounds while I was unemployed." Why? Food fights boredom and it is a common stress-buster. By overeating or overindulging, we limit our ability to perform successfully.

People who are unemployed spend more time eating because they have more time to do so. Going to the fridge or the cupboard is an easy, comforting break from whatever you're doing. Frequently, people turn to food to find a sense of fulfillment. We warn you though—lay off the burgers, fries, and pizza. Fast food makes you feel good for the moment, but look out for the rest of your day. You need your energy—now more than ever—and having abundant, quality fuel will make a difference. Food is often used to cope with emotional situations. There are several reasons people give for overeating:

- "Food isn't critical or judgmental."

- "Food makes me feel good now."

- "Food offers me comfort."

- "Food is always there."

No wonder people overeat! Food sounds like the perfect friend. In social relationships, we need good boundaries and rules to keep our friends supporting us. The same is true for our relationship with food. Generally speaking, however, it's okay to raid the fridge, but stock it with healthy snacks and foods. Here are some basic ways to avoid overeating:

- Eat a good breakfast to avoid overeating during lunch or dinner.

- Be aware of your body: eat only when you're hungry.
- Eat smaller portions throughout the day instead of large portions at mealtimes.
- Be aware of what you eat—keep a daily food diary.
- Get to know the foods that make you feel full longer during the day.
- Consult a nutritionist for finding your proper daily nutrition needs.
- Try not to grocery shop when you're hungry.
- Increase the ratio of vegetables to starches in your meals—it will make you feel full.
- Use a salad plate instead of a dinner plate for serving portions.
- Eat only at the dinner table and not in front of the TV, with a newspaper, or reading a book. You're likely to be unaware that you are full if your attention is focused on something other than your meal
- Plan each meal: breakfast, lunch, dinner, and snacks. Make a grocery list of the items you need and buy only items that are on the list.
- Drink more water and eat more water-based foods, such as vegetables and soups.
- Keep healthy snacks on hand.
- Exercise regularly—it helps reduce appetite.
- Get enough sleep so that your energy comes from rest and not food.
- Eat protein with every meal.
- Reduce the number of times you eat at fast-food restaurants and at other restaurants. Restaurant portions are typically larger than portions you need, and fast food is usually high in fat and calories.

There is a flip side to this equation—be aware that losing five, ten, or more pounds from lack of appetite and not eating could stem anywhere from simple stress to clinical depression. Loss of appetite doesn't necessarily mean you have clinical depression. It could be a simple response to the immediate increase of stress in your life.

As we mentioned above, we want to keep food as our good friend. We want to avoid denying ourselves something we need. Overeating is a problem in itself, but not eating enough can be just as dangerous. Even if you're not hungry, make sure that when you do eat, you make it count.

The basics of eating healthy do not have to be expensive; however, it is well worth spending a little more to buy foods that are better for you. During your time of unemployment, there is no need to go on a radical or fad diet. Good foods are often the foods that make you feel full anyway. You may also want to use this time to study basic nutrition guidelines or consult nutrition Web sites:

- The American Heart Association: **www.americanheart.org**
- The American Diabetes Association: **www.diabetes.org**
- United States Health and Human Services: **www.healthierus.gov**
- Food & Nutrition Information Center: **www.nal.usda.gov/fnic**
- United States Department of Agriculture: **www.nutrition.gov**

There are many excellent resources that tell you how to eat healthily. Remember that eating and eating well are critical components to maintaining your daily routine and a healthy sense of self.

LIMIT PERSONAL AND SOCIAL DRINKING

While under stress, many unemployed people often turn to drinking alcohol or other drug use. Drinking and having fun is part of many people's lives, but like anything else, moderation is the key. Alcohol is a depressant. That's a fact. Just like food, it can be improperly used as a crutch or coping strategy in dealing with the curve balls life throws us. Since unemployment can be one of life's most stressful events, this is a good time to monitor and manage your alcohol intake. We are not suggesting that you go on the wagon. Just drink responsibly and reduce the heavy binges. If you cut back on alcohol, you'll save money—that stuff isn't cheap!

Alcohol and other addictive drug use could rise during times of unemployment. If you've struggled in the past with addictive substances, it is especially important during this time that you see an addiction counselor and attend daily, weekly, or monthly support meetings. You'll be glad you did, as your future depends on you staying clean. If you or someone you know has a drinking problem, you can find further information at **www.alcoholics-anonymous.org,** or for drug abuse visit Narcotics Anonymous at **www.na.org.**

DROP-KICK BAD HABITS

Everyone has bad habits, vices, or shadow sides to their personalities. When we get stressed, we have a tendency to fall back into them. Why do we do this? As bad as they may be, they are still old and familiar comfort zones to help us cope with life.

- Do you smoke more?
- Have you increased your alcohol consumption?
- Do you eat too much or too little?
- Are you sleeping too late or not enough?
- Are you usually isolated from your family or friends?
- Do you exercise too much or too little?
- How many hours of television do you watch in a day?
- Do others easily irritate you?
- Are you short-tempered or even too obsessive?

Yep, when we get too stressed, Mr. Hyde can reappear and take over Dr. Jekyll.

Our indulgent properties too often become a destructive attempt to nurture ourselves. Strange as it seems, personal vices and mannerisms are hard to give up if you don't have anything to fill the void. These bad habits can cause us to quickly lose our personal and professional decorum and be hurtful to others and ourselves.

MY TEN WORST HABITS... As hard as it may be, take a few minutes to list ten bad habits that you would like to avoid falling back into while looking for your next job. If you have the courage, post them on the fridge for everyone to see. Others can help support you with managing them and even find humor in your old fall-back positions.

1. _____   6. _____

2. _____   7. _____

3. _____   8. _____

4. _____   9. _____

5. _____   10. _____

STEP AWAY FROM THE VIDEO GAMES!

When you start calling your kids or friends by your favorite action game superhero, it's time to put your hands in the air and step away from the video games. Just like any vice, video games, computer games, and Internet surfing can become addicting. In fact, there are mental health therapists and Web sites that deal with computer addiction. Here is a list of Web sites with information on Internet or video game abuse:

- www.netaddiction.com
- www.computeraddiction.com

Nobody likes to admit it, but when people appear to be perusing their handheld personal digital assistant or allege to be working on their computer, they are, in fact, sometimes playing solitaire and other games. Television, video games, and recreational Internet use are great but need to be managed.

These activities can increase a sense of isolation, drain energy, and decrease productivity while you are looking for a new job. Do yourself a favor and use them wisely.

Keep a log of how much time you spend each day on these activities. By tracking your time, this becomes the best manager of all. After tracking this for a week, month, or year, you'll be surprised at how much accumulated time is lost to these types of activities. Consider this: There are approximately 250 working days a year; if you spend 10 minutes a day each day for a year playing video games or aimlessly surfing the Net, that accumulates to nearly 42 hours, the equivalent of more than one regular working week!

INTERNET/VIDEO GAME ADDICTION QUIZ

	YES	NO
1. Do you find yourself spending more time on the Internet than expected?	☐	☐
2. Do you have trouble not playing video games for several days in a row?	☐	☐
3. Do you often check your e-mail before doing other things that must be done?	☐	☐
4. Is it difficult for you to limit the time you spend on the Internet?	☐	☐
5. Are you often thinking of the next time you'll be playing a video game or on the Internet?	☐	☐
6. Are you secretive when others ask what you are doing on the Internet?	☐	☐
7. Are you defensive if others tell you that you waste too much time playing video games?	☐	☐
8. Do you neglect personal hygiene or household chores to be on the Internet or playing video games?	☐	☐
9. Are you generally bored when not playing video games or visiting sites on the Internet?	☐	☐
10. Are your personal relationships suffering as a result of your Internet activity?	☐	☐

If you have answered "yes" to most of the questions above, you may want to consider cutting back the time you spend on the Internet or playing video games. Self-policing of your time is tough because it requires a lot of discipline and personal responsibility. Who can help if you think you have a problem? Put an alarm clock by your computer or hand over the controls to a family member or friend who says your time is up. Unemployment may not be the best time to become a professional video game master or Web surfer.

CHAPTER 4

EXPLORE YOUR SEVERANCE PACKAGE THOROUGHLY

TAKE STOCK IN YOUR FINANCES

If you are anticipating being laid off or if you just found out you will be, now is the time to begin thinking smartly about a few immediate financial steps that can save you headaches in the long run. First and most importantly, explore every option in your company's severance plan and be sure to ask for everything you want. Do not be shy, you have very little to lose.

- Check the status of your pension. Are you vested? Can the schedule for being fully vested be accelerated? If no, can you obtain additional cash in severance to cover this loss?

- Research options and rollover terms for any retirement or investment accounts.

- How long will your employee benefits last? Inquire if they last as long as your cash severance package does.

- Will your severance package cover other services such as continued access to a computer, e-mail, fax, and telephone, or provide assistance with preparing résumés and job coaching?

Once you've explored all your severance options, begin looking at all other immediate resources available:

- Schedule all medical and dental appointments while you still have employer-sponsored health insurance.

- Start checking group health insurance plans, including COBRA. Investigate availability and deadlines for applications.

- Look into individual policy options for your group life insurance plan.

- Be sure to claim your unemployment insurance as soon as you are eligible. It may not be much, but it will be better than receiving nothing at all. The United States Department of Labor (**www.workforcesecurity.doleta .gov/map.asp**) has links to every state unemployment office in the country.

- Call all your creditors and request modified repayment plans.

Now that you have addressed your most immediate financial needs, which require a more rapid response, you are now prepared to focus on other financial strategies that will assist you during this challenging time.

CHECK ON YOUR FINANCES

People often become energized and feel empowered when utilizing this time to re-evaluate and adjust their monthly budgets and overall living expenses. You can lower your expenses by taking the following steps:

- Compare rates for car insurance.

- Use low-cost public transportation.

- Take advantage of double-coupon day.

- Buy generic brands at the grocery store.

- Cancel your newspaper and magazine subscriptions and read them on the Internet or at the library.

- Fill your car's gas tank with cheaper gasoline.

- Transfer your credit card balance to a low-rate credit card (but get out of the habit of carrying any debt).

- Order from the $.99 menu rather than eating at expensive restaurants.

- Donate goods to charitable organizations. This is good for you and your charity of choice, as the charity gets your donations, and you create a worthy tax write-off (no matter how small).

- Adjust the amount of utilities you use.

- Water your lawn less.

- Fix any leaky faucets or annoying drips around the house.

- Use less electricity by turning off the lights when you're not in the room—the vacant furniture doesn't need them on.

- If you have an air conditioner, turn the thermostat up two or three degrees or turn your heater down in the winter and put on a sweater.

- Find the best local and long distance provider for your phone service.

- If you don't need your cell phone, turn it off and save on your bill.

- If the straits become dire, then find a new and cheaper place to live.

- Dump your expensive gym membership and find someplace less expensive to work out and socialize.

- Cancel satellite or cable television services.

All of these strategies will reduce your monthly utility costs and, surprisingly, many are also good for the environment! By lowering your cost of living, you can only decrease your anxiety about not having enough money and when you do find a job, you'll be able to take full advantage of further maximizing your dollar. Life isn't just about how much money you make, but about how you value and spend each and every dollar earned. Go ahead, live like a rock star on your newfound budget.

BUDGET THE BASICS

One of the most practical and immediate stress-busters is to develop a financial plan to commit to during times of limited financial resources. This plan should be something you and your family can work with. By sticking to the family budget rules, you'll avoid feeling wishy-washy over expensive spending opportunities or go unnecessarily into debt. If someone asks you to do something expensive, your reply should be: "Do we have a budget for that?"

Step 1:

Assess what you have coming in for income and know how much is in your checking and savings account.

Step 2:

Know where your money goes. This may be the most difficult part. If you are doing this, you're better off than most people. Most people do not realize how much money they spend in a day, week, or month. Do you leave the ATM with money in your pocket but by the end of the day you're often wondering where it all went? Keeping track of your money is difficult because it requires a lot of work to save your receipts, and it can create anxiety from the unpleasant surprise of seeing where your money goes and how much you actually spend. Save your receipts in a shoebox, envelope, or collator. Write totals down in an expense journal, use software packages, or even keep a handwritten ledger to track where every penny goes.

Step 3:

Set a realistic budget and include everything: rent or mortgage, car payment, house insurance, car insurance, health and dental insurance, gas for the car, car maintenance, natural gas for the house, heating oil, electricity, phone use, cable or satellite TV, water, sewer and garbage, Internet connection, cell phones, groceries, credit card payments, entertainment, vacation, and birthday and holiday expenses. You can even budget for a miscellaneous fund in case something comes up or if you want to have a little extra fun.

Step 4:

Create a savings and debt account for your family. Unemployment is a tough time to do this, but consider saving a percentage of your income for some savings (even if it's only $5) and pay down your debt. If it's too painful for you to transfer the money yourself (because you want to use it for something else), ask your bank to automatically transfer a certain amount each month for you and pretend the money was never there. In good times, it is not unusual while employed to always save 10 percent of all income. Have the 10 percent going toward unpaid debts and live on the remainder. If you struggle with doing this on your own, you can talk to your local bank, financial planner, or a highly recommended debt counselor.

Step 5:

Balance your checkbook at the end of the month and see how you did staying within your budget.

Once you've determined what you're spending money on and what you need to spend money on, deciding where to make cuts and how to budget the basic priorities should be a snap. Below is a sample worksheet for you to complete your family budget.

SAMPLE WORKSHEET

Add lines 2 and 3, then subtract from line 1. If you have a deficit, then you may need to reevaluate your family budget.

Monthly income:

Temporary employment income	$ _____
Severance check	$ _____
Unemployment check	$ _____
Savings draw	$ _____
1. Subtotal	$ _____

How much is put toward savings?

Savings	$ _____
Unpaid debt	$ _____
2. Subtotal	$ _____
3. Add total expenses	$ _____

This exercise is not meant to create worry and anxiety. It's a management tool to show you in black and white where you are financially. You can objectively use this information to determine how much you need and then get creative on how to bring in additional income.

PLAN AHEAD

You never know what tomorrow may bring (and you know this better than anyone). Pray that you never have to go through being unemployed again, but in case you do, it is best to apply the old Boy Scout motto, "Be Prepared." When working, it is better to plan ahead and live within your means—save your pennies for a rainy day.

There is a difference between living comfortably and living luxuriously. If you are in debt up to your eyeballs when an unfavorable wind blows, your entire world can come crashing down. Generally speaking, younger generations are notorious for thinking that bad days may never come. Unlike Americans who benefited from the experience of living through the depression and post–World War II eras, younger people are more comfortable with carrying large debt, driving expensive cars, keeping high mortgage payments, maintaining revolving credit card debt, and having no need for savings.

Planning ahead is just good business. If unemployment ever happens to you, your friends, or your family, the following basic suggestions might be helpful:

- While you're employed, live in a house, condo, or apartment that you can support if you should have to take this wonderful ride again.

- Keep your debt low. We tend to have spending habits with the belief that we will always have enough, so we run up our credit cards and debt ratios to buy expensive cars, clothes, and big-kid toys like boats, personal watercrafts, motorbikes, and all-terrain vehicles. If you have credit card debt, contact your creditors to arrange for lower payment plans until you find another job.

- If you know your layoff is coming and you will receive a severance pay package, think twice about how you spend it. There is always the temptation of instant gratification to fly off on an exotic vacation. But bear in mind that this source of funding is not limitless and it often takes longer to find employment than you expect.

- When employed, have a separate "unemployment" savings account that equals three to six months of normal pay that you do not touch in case you find yourself unemployed again. This is your own version of a severance plan.

- Start developing a food storage plan. Remember—Twinkies don't have a shelf life; they have a half-life of three to twelve months. Buying one or two extra cans of food each week for storage is perhaps the easiest method of all.

Planning ahead for the curve ball that life may throw you will always make the pitch easier to hit. Hopefully, that day will never come, but if it should, at least you'll be prepared to handle it.

Borrow Wisely from the Bank of Dad

If you ask friends or family for financial assistance in times of dire need, treat the transaction as you would a loan from any formal banking institution. Write a contract or promissory note that details the terms or repayment schedule. Include interest amounts and dates of each payment, the length of time on the note, and if possible, secure it against your car, your house, your dog, or your personal CD collection—something that shows good faith in the loan. Legitimizing the transaction on paper supports both the lender and borrower. Without this security, one of the parties runs the risk of feeling subordinate (borrower) or taken advantage of (lender). You can locate promissory notes and basic contracts at your local library, on the Internet, or from an attorney.

Borrowing from the Bank of Dad (or your friends and family) to get you through the tough times can be uncomfortable for both parties. This may place your friends or parents in an awkward situation financially or they may fall into a role of caretaker, provider, or guardian. (Keep in mind your parents may also be spending your inheritance already on something else.) It can be difficult for them to say yes or no to your request because of the personal relationship you maintain, but if handled properly, it can be a wonderful social process for both parties.

Ask Yourself: "What Is Wealth?"

The desires to obtain, preserve, and expand our material possessions dates back almost as far as history records. Today is no different. As a society, we haven't dropped the belief of measuring who we are by what we have. There are, however, many ways to measure wealth. Some people describe themselves as being wealthy when possessing great knowledge, family and friends, a comfortable place to hang their hat at the end of the day, spirituality, education, and many other prized experiences and characteristics of nonmaterial value.

Wealth is more descriptive when expanded beyond the limitations of mere dollars:

- Do you have an appreciation of art?

- Do you have a personal music collection or library?

- Do you maintain a garden?   • Are you writing in a journal?

- Do you have a strong sense of self?   • Are you self-reliant?

- Do you have a loyal pet?   • Do you have an education?

- Do you keep a scrapbook or family photo album?

- Do you appreciate beautiful surroundings?

- Do you play a musical instrument?

- Are you gifted with a beautiful singing voice?

- Do you have a good emotional support base of family and friends?
- Have you traveled and experienced many leisure adventures?
- Do you do good deeds for others?
- Do you take advantage of free time?
- Do you give to charity or the community?
- Do you find successes and lessons from your failures?
- Do you keep and value personal awards and certificates?
- Do you have a healthy body?
- Do you remember your fond memories often?
- Do you enjoy your proud heritage and political freedoms?

WHAT WEALTH IS TO ME... In addition to those listed above, take a moment to consider what things make you wealthy.

_____

_____

_____

_____

_____

Everybody is wealthy, whether you feel wealthy or not. When we are unemployed, we often get caught in the narrow view of feeling poor because of our financial status. But we are already wealthy beyond our wildest dreams; we just need to take the time to discover why.

HOME-MADE GOOD-NESS

IMPROVE YOUR SURROUNDINGS

Now is a great time (because you have it) to restore some organization and order to your life. Many times we are so busy during our workweek that we overlook the care of our surroundings. This is the time to bring order to your life and household and to begin checking things off a to-do list:

- Clean out the closets and give away old clothes.

- Take your dried-up Christmas tree, which has been sitting in the corner of the room for six months, to the dump.

- Clean out the fridge—start by throwing out old salad dressing bottles that have an inch of dressing left, and toss the two-year-old pasta sauce that's certain to give you a nice case of botulism.

- Organize the garage.

- Clean your car and house.

- Read that book that has been sitting on your shelf collecting dust.

- Reconnect with an old friend or family member.

- E-mail friends or write letters to people you used to know in places you used to live.

- Revise or get a will and a power of attorney. Get a free Advance

Directives Packet from your local hospital (living will, medical power of attorney, etc.).

- In addition, you and your family should know the status and location of all of your accounts, including checking, savings, retirement, safe deposit boxes, and wills.

You'll feel better for having accomplished something productive and you'll have added order to your life.

I'VE BEEN MEANING TO . . . . This is also an excellent time to improve the surroundings of your house, to keep your living environment nice and neat. Too often we let our immediate surroundings deteriorate in a hurry. Write down ten things you've been meaning to do (or your spouse has been meaning for you to do).

1. _____   6. _____
2. _____   7. _____
3. _____   8. _____
4. _____   9. _____
5. _____   10. _____

Your home is your castle
(or oasis), so make your kingdom a comfortable place to clear your head after a hard day—employed or not. Besides, even royalty needs downtime. If your home isn't already comfortable, this is the time to make some economical home improvements.

Make Your Home an Oasis

- Bring in some plants.

- Paint the walls a nice color, or even paint the house a new color.

- Rearrange your furniture.

- Hang pictures or paintings on your walls.

- Improve the lighting.

- Reduce clutter.

- Play background music.

- Make the house smell good with candles, incense, or potpourri.

- Add a small indoor water fountain.

- Plant a garden and enjoy vegetables throughout the summer.

Take a moment and think of other ideas to help make your home more of an oasis and transform your abode into a place to relax and escape from the stresses of the daily grind.

LET KIDS BE KIDS

Losing your job is tough enough, but telling your family might be even tougher. People often ask if they should tell their children, and if so, how and when? Most importantly, you want to be truthful about what has happened and let them know the changes that are to come. Try not to wait too long to make the announcement. The actual telling, though, may take some grace and finesse.

If you don't know how to do this, watch the evening news. Like any great newscaster, telling the bad news is all in the delivery. There is no need to dramatize it; the news will speak for itself. If your emotions are running high, take some time to compose yourself. Gather everyone around for a family meeting and make the announcement as matter-of-factly as possible. "Earlier today, I learned my company is making changes that will affect all of us. Starting (fill in the day), I will no longer be working there. There's no need to worry because I'm taking steps to make sure that everyone will be fine. We'll make it together." You can fill in all the remaining details you wish and then take questions from your family members as if they were reporters. Be sure to stay calm, clear, and concise in your answers, reaffirming you are in charge of the situation and that all will soon be well.

Your message needs to be age-appropriate for all your family members, as children have different levels of emotional and intellectual development than adults. If you decide to tell young children, using games or stories to share the news will work great since they tend to process information best on that level. Generally speaking, younger children tend to fear losing their home, going hungry, needing clothes, or the family breaking apart. Preteens and young adults often respond better through direct and ongoing communication during this difficult time. You can also offer support by helping to draw them out from time to time with questions and comments such as "Any worries?" or "Tell me more about what concerns you." They may have similar fears like their younger siblings, but often they add more practical concerns of not having financial support for things like extracurricular activities, college, weddings, or other financial commitments you may have.

Your children's eyes will be watching you during this time of change, so it is important to set a good example. No matter how competent or incompetent you may feel as a parent, your kids want to be like you—good or bad. You are making impressions all the time. Knowing this, what do you want to teach your children? If they were walking out the door today for the last time, what skills would you like your children to have—especially during times of stress?

- Optimism

- Respect of others—especially to your spouse

- Exhibit faith in life, that all will be okay in the long run

- Work as a team

- Have fiscal responsibility

- Have fun daily
- Exhibit empathy and kindness
- Take care of their physical health

I'D LIKE MY CHILDREN TO . . . Take a moment to fill in the blanks below of any life skills that you'd like your children to employ.

_____

_____

_____

_____

_____

_____

Once you've completed the list above, you have created your own road map to follow. By following it, you will teach your children by example—the most important strategy of all. You have to own these life skills yourself before you can model it for them, for they tend to watch what you do, rather than what you say.

If you don't set a good example, children may run a higher risk of taking on your adult worries. In fairness, some children still may take on adult worries or pick up a caretaker role no matter what you do, so do your best to discourage this dynamic from happening. Let your children know by words and actions that you are taking care of the new challenges ahead so they don't have to worry. Let your kids be kids.

Stick Together

Late in life many people regret not having spent more time with their family and friends. Not often will they wish they had spent more time at work. How many times do you hear people complain about not having enough time to spend with their spouse, children, or friends? There are many parents who, looking back at their unemployment time, find it was enjoyable to share more time with their kids, and their children also liked spending more time with their parents.

In times of stress, couples and families need to stick together. Money is one of the most influential factors in marital difficulties. When the economy is in a downswing, divorce rates rise. Both spouses are likely experiencing enormous disappointment, perhaps social embarrassment, and other external pressures.

Sadly, couples and families can become divided rather than pull together during difficult times. Emotional deficiencies and poor coping strategies become magnified. If you need assistance coping, seek counseling. There are many inexpensive avenues for receiving therapy. Use these options. If you stick together, you'll make it as a family/couple.

The choice is yours. This can be a time when your family pulls together, combines resources, and functions as a team to face this challenge, or a time when it breaks apart at the seams. If you have children, know you are being watched on how you handle adversity. There are some strategies that may make all the difference in holding these relationships together. Have a family activity together once a week. Find an hour or more in your busy schedules and go for ice cream, play games, read a book, make dinner and eat together, go for a walk, or watch a video. A weekly family meeting works very well for some families. It doesn't have to be lengthy—ten to twenty minutes can be enough time to allow your family to discuss what is happening in their lives, to plan for the week, or to assign chores.

If you're married or in a committed relationship, you should go on a date once a week. You don't need to discuss anything related to your unemployment or financial difficulties. Take a break. There will be plenty of time for responsible discussions later. This is a good time for recommitting to your relationship and cementing your partnership with one another. Don't let (a lack of) money stop you; go on a no-cost/low-cost date.

For singles who have no children, unemployment is different. You essentially have to only take care of yourself; however, there are still relationships to maintain with friends and loved ones. Singles with children have to make time to care for and nurture their kids while still looking for work; a challenging task when there is no partner for support. Whatever your situation may be, make time to spend with those you care about most. In return, you'll be grateful for their love and support during unemployment.

ENJOY NEW ROLES

The face of the American workforce has changed dramatically in the past several decades. The dynamic where one parent stayed at home as the primary caregiver for the children while the other worked full time to provide for the family is no longer the norm. More typically in today's society, both parents find themselves employed full or part-time to make ends meet.

But for those not used to this new daily reality when you lose your job, making the transition from full-time workaholic to full-time stay-at-home parent can be like landing in a foreign country where you don't speak the language. The culture shock can be immense. The world around you is suddenly different. There are no lunches or water cooler gatherings to talk about last night's television show or the big game on Sunday. Instead of time cards, team meetings, or business plans, there are now car pools, housecleaning, and play groups. Using your work lingo, acronyms, and phrases are now meaningless. At times, you'll be missing adult conversation. You'll crave intellectual stimulation besides the latest cartoon adventure song. The first time you take your children to the park may be like the first time you went as a youngster. "Will the other kids' parents like me?" "Will we have anything in common to talk about?"

The best way to handle your new situation is to be confident with your new role. How? Keep your sense of humor and enjoy the new opportunities:

- Become more involved with your children's lives. Have fun being the trailblazer in your neighborhood activities or leading school programs; be a carpool leader or a coach for your children's sports teams.

- Volunteer to escort a field trip.

- Swap cleaning tips from the other parents at the park.

- Organize a toy-swap program.

- Find out how to properly use that power tool in your garage.

- Organize activity circles for hobbies or interests of other stay-at-home parents: recipe club, construction group, card games, knitting circle, etc.

- Get to know the Web sites, newsletters, and conferences that are directed at supporting stay-at-home parents.

- Since men and women have different parenting skills unique to them, this is a great opportunity to teach your child some of your own qualities or skills. Ask yourself, "What can I teach my child?"

Stay-at-home parents often feel they are developing bonds with their children that they wouldn't normally have the opportunity to form if they had a full-time job. Unfortunately, being isolated and finding resources or support can make working from home even tougher. There are online references for stay-at-home parents that serve as useful resources and networks for both mothers and fathers. These sites often include ideas for family fun, helpful articles, news, books, and an extensive collection of links. When one parent is home during the day with the children, that person often forgets that their spouse doesn't have it so easy either:

- Are they coping with disappointment of having to work?
- Could they be feeling "mom" or "dad withdrawal" from not seeing the family?
- Do they believe they are not a good parent because of being at work during the day?

Visit these Web sites to get information about stay-at-home dads and moms:

- Slowlane: www.slowlane.com
- Cincinnati Dads: www.cincinnatidads.com
- Fathers First: www.fathersfirst.org
- The National Association of At-Home Mothers: www.athomemothers.com
- At Home Moms: www.athomemoms.com
- The Light Keeper: www.thelightkeeper.com

For the parent at home, help facilitate your partner's time with your children each day to help honor them as mom or dad. Fighting the stigma of being a stay-at-home parent or being out of work is largely a matter of your own perspective. It can be fun or awkward. Go ahead and call your new role domestic genius, goddess, or engineer. You'll learn quickly that one parent staying at home happens more often than you think (especially for men), even if it's not by your choice at this time.

Appreciate the new chance you've been given to experience a different side of your life. Most importantly, remember your job is to do what is best for the family in any given situation. How it looks is up to you.

GET OUT! YOUR FAMILY AND DOG WILL THANK YOU

Obviously, it's important to have dedicated time to focus your attention and efforts on finding a job. Oftentimes, your living arrangements provide too many distractions and don't offer a productive work setting. Get out of the house. Find a place to go where you can be more productive. In the long run, this might be what you need to keep you and your family members from saying or doing anything you or they might regret later.

- Go to a public or college library where you'll have a quiet place to work, space for meetings and groups, plus Internet access and other potential resource materials.

- Conduct job research and keep current with newspapers and periodicals.

- If you have a little money saved up, you may want to rent an office for a minimal monthly fee. Leasing companies are typically delighted to have some money from a tenant rather than leaving a space empty.

- Inquire with friends if they have a "spill-over" office in their building or suite of offices not currently in use. This may land you an inexpensive or even free solution for daily job hunting.

- Some states' Department of Workforce Services have facilities to provide you with desk space and access to a phone, a fax, a copier, and the Internet. You may also see other complimentary services offered, such as résumé writing, interviewing, personal budgeting, and job fair notification. Most states vary in what is offered, but it's definitely worth investigating.

Having just said, "Get out of the house," you may be surprised at the next suggestion. Establish a designated home office. If you don't already have an office at your disposal, now is an excellent time to get one. Not only are home offices less expensive than renting office space, if done correctly, they may provide you with a home office deduction with the IRS. Be warned though—working from home has its own challenges. It can be isolating, as you have no colleagues with whom to interact. Also, you must establish clear boundaries and rules while working from home. When you are in your (home) office, you are working. Be firm about no unscheduled visits from friends, or even your spouse (but do it nicely). If your budget allows, install a separate phone line to take business calls and search the Internet. Being at home also offers a lot of other distractions. Temptations such as the television, refrigerator, and hobbies can be hard to resist. Numerous books and magazines will offer more in-depth guidance on how to best work from home, but these suggestions should get you started with a new home office.

LIVING AT THE HOTEL MOM

In much of American culture, the greatest sign of individual independence is the day we move out of our parents' house and into our own living space. This ranks right up there with the day you obtain your driver's license— what a wonderful sense of freedom! This is why checking back into the "Hotel Mom" can be such a culture shock if your needs require it.

A major theme of this book and discussion is to utilize all the resources available: physical, emotional, spiritual, financial, and intellectual. Receiving help from friends and family for some of our basic necessities such as food and shelter can be a wonderful opportunity to spend time with those you love, save money, or reconnect with old relationships. Of course, once the happy reunion is over, moving in with friends or family has its own pit-falls. The first time a parent asks you what time you'll be home or tells you your child needs different disciplining, you'll feel there isn't enough money in the world to get you to stay or not pitch a tent in the backyard.

All families have their own rules and expectations when living together. Beware, the rules when you were a child or a teenager may still be in effect. It can be difficult for parents to treat you any other way, especially in their own house, no matter how much education you have or what your station in life is. Remember that old roles and new rules will eventually show up. When you come together, you may need to come up with a new set of guidelines or family bylaws that outline clear rules and expectations to help facilitate more harmony in the home. These rules can make living with friends and family a more enjoyable experience and keep you from jumping out the window on the worst days.

A few strategies or suggestions outlined below can help you stay an equal player with an equal vote in the new home and keep you from feeling you've been cast in the latest reality TV show called *Mom and Dad, I'm back!*

- When coming together for a temporary merger, have an up-front discussion to set clear expectations, rules, and boundaries for living in the home. Everything from where you park your car to TV time, computer time, conserving utilities, phone use, kitchen access, meals together, and areas that are off-limits to you. These should be written down and discussed thoroughly. Turn this discussion into a common set of rules or bylaws like any good business. Once the rules are drawn up, everyone signs and everyone gets a copy.

- Discuss rent payment. What is the expectation? Is money going to be exchanged and if so, how much and when. If not, offer services such as yard work, maintenance, car repair, chauffeuring, or lending personal expertise. Just because you're moving back into the family house doesn't mean it should be treated like a free ride. No matter how tight money is, paying something for rent is how you stay as an equal player, helps avoid old roles, and facilitates a way to own your seat and not feel subordinate to living in someone else's domain. Even paying one of the monthly bills will make you feel much better. Pay the gas, electric, or water bill, buy the groceries for a week of cooking, man the house so your friends or family can go out for the night or weekend. It can be a mutual exchange that supports everyone. You can save money while your parents receive something in return—additional company and easing their financial burdens or lack of time.

- Set aside one hour a week for a house meeting. Like any good business, host a regular staff meeting on ways to improve the living process for everyone. Call it the "Family Business Meeting," the "Dirty Laundry Club," or the "Kitchen Cabinet." This meeting time is not just about airing disappointments or things under your skin, but is also about discussing how to improve the household processes.

- Support you, the individual. One of the toughest parts of communal living is finding ways to feel like an individual in a larger social process. Try to find your own personal space or get out of the house and enjoy the things you like to do. Get a headset and listen to your favorite music as loud as you want. Find a place outside to hang up a hammock or get up early to have free rein of the house—bathrooms, kitchen, your favorite reading chair, or extra quiet time. Get a do-not-disturb sign for your door. Park your car down the street so your parents don't know you are there. Use the back door whenever possible. Get out your label gun for all your stuff in the fridge. Decorate your room or corner of the home with your stuff—from old rock-n-roll posters to the feng shui fountain.

- Support your marriage. If you are living in this space with your spouse, finding time alone with them outside the family home is critical. You both still need to support each other with one-on-one time.

- Support your children. The same goes for your children; individual parent/child date nights will help with their sanity, too.

- Blend family traditions. If you've been living alone, or with your own family, you can incorporate with or learn new traditions from your new hosts. This time is a great opportunity to blend family traditions—share cooking and meals, start and complete projects, or partake in musical activities. If Thursday night in your old house was pizza or Mexican food night, share the tradition in your new living situation. Have fun and be flexible to your hosts' requests for involvement in their traditions or tribunals as well.

- Like an extended stay in a hotel, this visit is temporary until you get back on your feet again. From the beginning, develop an exit strategy, a plan for leaving when the time is right or when you don't feel it's working for you any longer. If it helps, set a time frame to live there or a trial period to see if it will work. No matter how things go—good, bad, or awful—always be grateful to your friends and family for making themselves available to provide a communal living process for you. When the day comes for you to check out, have a farewell party to offer thanks for a gracious host.

There is no shame in moving back in with your parents or with your friends for a while. Honor yourself and honor your host's commitment to your time of need.

CHAPTER 6

CONDENSED INGREDIENTS

AVOID ISOLATION: IT'S SO . . . ISOLATING

A common pitfall while you're unemployed is to become isolated from your friends and family. Most likely, many of them will be employed during the period you are between jobs. Besides embarrassment, another reason that unemployed people tend to isolate themselves from their friends is because they no longer have extra money to go out for a burger, to attend movies and concerts, or to take trips. It can feel like an awkward situation believing you are not able to "go along" with the crowd and do what they do. But, there's nothing embarrassing about it. Be clear that you want to be included in their activities, but also let it be known what you can and can't afford. Don't be ashamed if you can't join them every time. Trust us, though: they do want to have you with them. In some situations, your friends may even chip in to help you out. Don't be embarrassed to accept their offer—we all need a little assistance sometimes. And if it makes you anxious, don't worry—someday you'll return the favor. Look over the following questions to see if you are isolating yourself:

1. Do you lack intimate bonds with others?

2. Do you not feel the need to be involved in a romantic relationship?

3. Do you wish you had more friends?

4. Do you feel overwhelmed at the thought of going out to meet new people?

5. Do you turn down invitations to be with other people?

6. Do you feel that if you don't have a job, others will find you less desirable to be around?

7. Have you chosen to live far away from family and friends?

8. Do you live alone?

9. Do you feel like you're doing fine by yourself and you don't need anyone else?

10. Are there people you'd like to see, meet, or call but are reluctant to initiate contact?

Your family and friends may not be able to get you a job, but they'll be able to help you with your well-being while you're looking for one. They want to see you succeed as much as you do.

Tell the Truth—It Will Set You Free

Socializing is an important process during your unemployment tenure. Here are some great ways to spend time with your friends, family, or colleagues:

- Host a potluck dinner at home.

- Have people over for home-decorating TV show night.

- Check out classic old movies from the library and invite your colleagues and friends over. Ask them to prepare their favorite appetizer or dessert, and you can serve iced tea and lemonade.

- Host a penny-and-nickel poker game night.

- Get the gang together to watch the big game.

- For get-togethers, make your own salsa, buy chips, serve inexpensive drinks, and allow your pals to bring the good stuff.

- Create a book club or a hobby group for scrapbook or quilting.

It is a great moment when someone tells you the truth about their situation, void of any embarrassment, humiliation, or anxiety. Telling people you're unemployed is okay. There is no shame—it happens to millions of Americans every year. In fact, in most circumstances, your joblessness may not be entirely your fault and may have nothing to do with you whatsoever. Do you often find yourself lying or repressing the truth about your unemployment? There's no reason to be embarrassed when you speak the truth. There's a difference in speaking from a truthful, authoritative stand-point versus speaking as a victim or from a self-conscious position.

Benefits of Telling the Truth

- Greater opportunities for success in life

- Increased sense of personal confidence and self-satisfaction

- Being trusted by others

- Less anxiety, worry, and guilt

- Ability to solve problems and handle personal challenges

- Stronger interpersonal relationships

- Greater emotional health and control of your emotions

- Better physical health and the ability to sleep more comfortably at night

- Increased ability to think clearly and for greater self-expression

- Improved sense of humor

When someone asks what you are doing, say "I'm unemployed" or "I'm look-ing for work. It's a great business." If your financial troubles require you to move back home, then go ahead and say, "I'm unemployed, and I live with my parents." If it makes your conversation partner feel uncomfortable, then that's too bad. They can deal with it on their own time. How you speak of your current situation makes all the difference to your listener and, ulti-mately, to your self-image. Go ahead—tell the truth, it will set you free.

LAUGH IT UP! IT'S THE BEST MEDICINE OF ALL!

Sometimes a situation like this may seem so overwhelming that it almost feels like a soap opera or a melodrama. Please know that your life is not an episode of *As the Sofa Spins*. At a time like this, you need to keep your perspective and your sense of humor.

Benefits of Laughter

- Balances the immune system
- Lowers blood pressure
- Increases joy and happiness
- Is equivalent to cardiovascular activities like rowing or jogging
- Releases negative emotions
- Improves creativity
- Increases vascular blood flow and oxygenation of the blood
- Relaxes muscles
- Reduces stress hormones

There's a noticeable difference in people who find humor in their daily challenges versus those who constantly worry, express self-pity, and act like a victim in the face of daily challenges. Under any circumstance, life is too short to lose your sense of humor. Find opportunities for conversations and activities that are amusing. Be careful of watching other people's problems in soap operas, dramas, or depressing news stories. People who are unemployed oftentimes sit at home with the television on all day, watching soap operas, 24-hour news channels, or "B" movies that went straight to video. A lot of television programming includes depressing stories that are used for shock value, or stories that are just plain bad. Watch the evening news to stay informed, but beyond that, avoid too much television.

- Try reading and exchanging those witty e-mails that you never had time to write
- Get back to reading comics and watching cartoons
- Try to see the humor in any situation
- Go to funny movies

- Make fun of yourself

- Decorate your refrigerator or bulletin board with funny pictures, comic strips, and sayings

- Tell jokes to your friends over lunch or coffee

Laughing is a wonderful, endorphin-producing activity. Best of all, it spreads easily and is self-perpetuating. Keep your current situation in perspective, but try not to take it so seriously that you forget the best medicine of all—laughter.

FIND SUPPORTIVE PEOPLE

Seek out people who create positive energy. There's no reason to go through life or difficult situations alone. People move us outside ourselves, support us, and may offer insights that we miss on our own. There's often an unwarranted shame or embarrassment involved with having lost your job. People who are out of work have a tendency to isolate themselves from friends and family and to shy away from potential sources of support. Having a strong social support base is an enormous strength at any time in your life, but it's an especially important coping strategy when you're unemployed.

Surround yourself with people who will support you during this strenuous and disappointing time. Hang out and do what you would normally do with your friends if you were employed. Try to meet people who have been in the same situation. Talk to them about what they did to cope and how they handled it. You'll feel less isolated, less embarrassed, and less alone in your grief. Be wary of hanging with people who are real downers, even if only for a moment. Save your energy—it's a precious resource. Only spend it with those who don't rob you of it. People to generally avoid are those with poor attitudes who feel like victims or who struggle with being optimistic and enthusiastic about life. Tell them in a polite way that you are not available to hang out with them for awhile, and don't feel guilty about it.

You can also seek out professional clergy or other spiritual advisors. In addition to providing comfort or guidance, they're free. Also, it may be important to talk with professional therapists. Therapy is often perceived as very expensive; however, local churches will often subsidize or pay entirely for professional counseling. In many communities there are counseling programs that charge flat minimal fees or on a sliding scale based on your income.

CREATE A SUPPORT GROUP

Create a support group. Many people would welcome having a group of interested people with whom to discuss the difficulties and hardships of their situation, but they generally don't know such a group. Well, you most likely won't find one sitting at home. Although meeting with your friends for coffee on a regular basis is a great start, you'll create a helpful synergy by expanding your network and conversation to include people who are struggling with the same circumstances. This type of group will help you find humor during your time of duress and pain, decrease feelings of shame, and also help remind you that your unemployment is not your fault.

DO FOR OTHERS

Sometimes unemployment can be very self-centered. We focus all our time and energy on ourselves, or only the immediate needs of our families. Of course this is important, but don't

How to Start an Unemployment Support Group

1. Make flyers: print your name and a time and location of where to meet.

2. Post flyers in libraries, cafés, unemployment offices, coffee shops, and grocery stores.

3. Make a schedule to meet on a regular basis.

4. Exchange phone numbers or e-mail addresses in case changes in schedules occur.

5. Take advantage of collective resources, share coping strategies, swap unemployment stories and interview nightmares.

6. Present résumés to each other and give feedback.

7. Give updates about interviews completed.

get caught up spending all of your time in fear and anxiety over the sheer responsibility of it all. Get outside of yourself and do something kind for someone else. You'll feel better. Find ways to do something for other people on a daily, weekly, or monthly basis:

- Volunteer for a local community activity or help clean an elderly neighbor's yard.

- Make a quick phone call to others and brighten their day.

- Visit a nursing home or your local hospital and volunteer even a small amount of your time.

- Ask a religious leader how to become more involved with church or charities.

- Donate your time to community gardens, local food banks, or homeless shelters.

- Though your money is tight, give your change or a couple of dollars to an individual or an organization in need.

- Volunteer at art galleries and museums, or the theater, opera, or symphony.

- Take time to tutor elementary children at a local school or community center.

- Become a Big Brother or Big Sister.

- Deliver meals to the elderly.

- Join community conservation groups.

Keep in mind that even though you won't be able to do this all day, even fifteen minutes a day or one evening a week is enough to help someone in need. As a bonus, your attitude and energy will be enhanced while you search for a job. Sometimes the greatest gift we have is our time, and now is an opportunity to share it with those in need.

SPEND TIME WITH FRIENDS—YOUR OTHER FAMILY

Now is your opportunity to spend quality time with those who mean the most to you. No more excuses. Generally speaking, we have two support bases: our immediate family members and our friends. One group you were born with, and the other you chose. In times of great need, your friendships have never been more important. The value of friendship is more than just the get-togethers; it's the e-mails, phone calls, and face-to-face conversations. It's the sharing of good times and bad, joys and sorrows. In most cases, our family members are limited, but our friend base is expansive. Take advantage of your availability and use the time wisely. It's understandable to be respectful of others' time and commitments, but do enjoy the time you have to share with them.

Simply put, your friends are not your family. This can be an asset because friends can utilize their independent wisdom when sharing in your disappointments and life experiences. Friends have skills and availability that your family does not. Friends are more likely to provide you with realistic and honest feedback than your family. Your family members are more likely to be *too* supportive of you by getting enmeshed in your problems. Friends have the ability to maintain a separateness from you and your problems that offers a different type of social support than family. A true friend is someone who may not agree with you or buy into your point of view, but he or she might offer an alternative perspective and has a better chance of not getting lost in your personal experience. They may provide you with a semblance or perspective of independence. They like the jokes you tell and have gone through a lot of good times with you.

In addition to the people you see now, reconnecting with old friends, old classmates, old teammates, old jobs, and previous towns where you've lived reminds you of good times and is an energy-producing experience. Get together and talk about the glory days, the old gang, and the good times that have gone by. Friends are forever, no matter the time or distance. When the reconnection is made, even with an old acquaintance, you'll find you pick up right where you were when you last left off. There are cool people in your life right now, and you have a unique opportunity to spend time with them.

HOST A PARTY FOR AN UNEMPLOYED FRIEND

Whether it's putting a few extra pennies in the "take one" cup at the convenience store or finding that special gift to commemorate a big event in your best friend's life, freely giving yourself is one of the most enjoyable experiences we can have. Gifts are offered at weddings and graduations. New mothers may receive weeks of food and diapers from neighbors or family. Even in the face of bad news, such as a death in the family or a neighbor facing a difficult medical challenge, we find ways to support these people with casserole suppers and small donations.

There is a lot of wisdom in the examples above. For those of you who are employed or who have recently returned to the workforce, you may want to consider the following suggestion: If you know someone who has recently lost his or her job and is struggling to make ends meet, why not facilitate or host an unemployment party for that person? There is a new and unique trend growing in the United States for friends and relatives to host such a gathering. A word of caution: If you are the one who is unemployed, it may be difficult for you to ask for or have a party for yourself. But if a friend or a relative makes the offer, go ahead and give it a try. Once you begin working again, you will then become the perfect facilitator or host for a friend, colleague, or relative because you can empathize with what they're going through.

For the organizer, make the event a surprise party or a planned event, just like a birthday party or wedding shower. Make it fun! After all, everyone loves a good party. Have the guests bring something the honoree can use: a package of toilet paper, food for their pet, pre-paid phone cards, a bus pass, gift certificates, or packaged meals that can be frozen for future dinners. In their time of need it is important to show them you care about their well-being. If they are finding it difficult to accept this generosity, have them read the "Learn to Receive" section in this chapter on page 76.

Hopefully, if the need ever arises, your friends will demonstrate the same kind of support you showed them and return the favor.

HONOR HOLIDAYS, BIRTHDAYS, AND ANNIVERSARIES

Unfortunately, our society has become good at celebrating events and relationships materialistically. Holidays, birthdays, anniversaries—you name it—the calendar is loaded with gift-giving occasions, and the retail world stands ready and waiting to accept your money. Even if you have a sound perspective on the purpose of these occasions, it's difficult to maintain your sanity while the neighbor's kids are showing off their new presents to your kids. For the most part, holidays and special events are about peace, goodwill, love, thankfulness, and relationships. Rather than giving gifts, give good deeds to one another—and give the greatest gift of all: your time.

Having said that though, presents really are great, and for very small costs you can still honor people with gifts. Here are a few suggestions for when money is tight:

- Create a homemade coupon book filled with free lawn care, car washes, baby-sitting services, walks, dinner preparation, and even free back rubs.

- Buy inexpensive, discounted gifts throughout the year and use them for birthdays and holidays as the need arises.

- Shop during seasonal closeouts during the off-season and other promotional times. Also, you'd be surprised at what you can find at dollar stores, bargain wholesalers, flea markets, and yard sales.

It can be easy to feel heavily burdened (not to mention indebted) for gift-giving throughout the year, but with a little creativity and ingenuity, you don't have to blow your rent money to honor the relationships you value. Go ahead, have fun, and celebrate!

LEARN TO RECEIVE

Believe it or not, the world needs more receivers than givers. It's easy to give. You feel better about yourself having done it. It's surprising how difficult it is for people to receive generosity, especially those who are typically the greatest givers. So often, people are resistant to receiving. Words such as "leech," "mooch," and "user" are terms thought of when somebody allows others to lend assistance by way of money, time, expertise, or talents. These types of responses rob us of personal connections to other people. Seriously, it's easy to learn to give and receive. If you have a friend in need, you help out because the time will come when you'll rely on their generosity to get you out of your tricky situation. As the saying goes, what goes around comes around.

Don't let your pride get in the way of other people's generosity, especially in times of need. There's a graciousness and sensitivity that benefits both the giver and the receiver. We need each other. When friends or family offer to buy a pizza or pay for medical expenses, counseling, food, gas, or other basic necessities of life, allow them to do it. It's simply them pulling you out of the mud, and if the tables were turned, you would pull them out too.

CHAPTER 7

WORK NO-BRAINER JOBS

Having some income is better than no income. Whatever your job was before, whether you were a high-paid executive or a medium-wage factory worker, give yourself permission to seek employment "below" your abilities. It will provide you with immediate income, potential health benefits, daily structure, social interaction, new skills, new acquaintances, and much-needed diversion while you search for what you really want to do.

A no-brainer job for one person may not be the same for another. It may not be as challenging as your most recent employment, but it is simple for you to do. It may have different types of challenges or utilize previous skills you have mastered. It can be something fun that doesn't cause you stress. Perhaps it is even best fitted to your hobbies or personal interests where you may be able to learn new skills or receive an employee discount on goods or services for your favorite activity.

There's value in your work no matter what job you perform. After being laid off, many people recognize that their "no-brainer" job was one of their favorite ways to spend the day. In short, it's enough to take pride in a job well done, even if you are earning less than ever before. Enjoy an honest day's pay for an honest day's work.

Consider Income Alternatives

The sign on a small table by a roadside reads, "Lemonade $.25." When we were kids and wanted to augment the allowance we had from our parents, many of us set up shop for ourselves with our own lemonade stand on those hot summer days. It was the budding youth of entrepreneurship. When we were teenagers, some of us worked early morning paper routes, offered baby-sitting services to the neighbors, or mowed lawns. In high school there were fund-raising drives for the band with candy sales, bake sales, and dollar car washes. In college, some of us went as far as throwing weekend parties with a $5 cover charge to help pay the rent. By the time we reach adulthood, these activities often go by the wayside in the name of pride and societal complicity, though they remain a part of our nostalgic youth.

We're not suggesting you set up shop with your old lemonade stand, but we are encouraging you to think outside the box to help provide a little extra in your time of need. At this juncture of your life, you may not feel you have much to offer, but you do have time, experience, and skill. Be creative. Working for trade has been in existence since before money was invented. Trade your time, skills, and expertise for goods or services. Investigate barter networks online (just keep in mind, there may be tax consequences for this, so consult your tax advisor if you do). If you are an artisan by hobby (or profession), such as a photographer, sculptor, painter, or quilter, put some of your work up for sale, or trade your services for something you need. Host your own backyard chili cook-off for your neighbors and friends. To earn a little extra cash, investigate teaching adult education classes in your field of expertise at the local community college. Better yet, clean out the garage and closets full of all that old stuff you've been collecting and hold a yard sale.

Just like when you were young, having a little extra in your pocketbook during your time of need can be fun, not to mention financially rewarding. There is no embarrassment or shame for putting yourself out there. Do we dare paraphrase the old cliché, "If life gives you lemons, sell lemonade."

ADD NEW JOB SKILLS

Learning new skills isn't only practical but will assist you in finding a new job and will create new opportunities. New skills give you a sense of empowerment. Take the time to learn or improve computer skills and new software programs. Learn to write better and to speak more comfortably in public. Learn about basic accounting and bookkeeping. No matter what your field, you'll enhance your marketability for future employment by learning or improving these skills.

Most employment Internet sites that market jobs offer education and career development sections. In addition, many junior colleges, universities, business schools, local high schools, and community centers offer continuing education classes in business, languages, humanities, and the arts. There may be costs associated with taking these courses, so make sure you invest in the most valuable classes for you. Try a woodworking class, learn a new instrument, study the history of a part of the world you know nothing about, learn a new language, take an auto repair and maintenance class, learn to fix yard sprinklers, or study landscape design. If you've had an aversion to accounting, learn something about it. Whatever your choice, this is an opportunity to acquire job skills in fields that are not currently related to your employment but will diversify your abilities, increase your sense of self-reliance, and improve your professional standing and marketability.

JUMP-START YOUR ENERGY LEVEL

Sometimes our physical and emotional batteries are just dead and we need a jump start. Today, you may want to look for work but might be lacking the energy to do so.

We discussed the importance of food in Chapter 3, but there are wonderful books and health magazines at your local library that can give you ideas for quick energy boosts as well as those things that take it away.

How do you get going if you have no energy?

- Take a ten- to thirty-minute nap
- Go for a short walk
- Call a friend who makes you feel better
- Splash cold water on your face
- Eat something that gives you a boost
- Read a favorite quote or affirmation
- Review past accomplishments and lessons learned
- Exercise
- Read something funny

MAKE THE BEST OF BEING OVERQUALIFIED

"I know I can do that job." "I could do that job in my sleep." "I can handle that job with one arm tied behind my back." These are common expressions while you're looking for your next job, but if you know this, chances are, so do the people hiring. It can be discouraging to hear "You're overqualified for the position" or "We can't afford you." This is both frustrating and disappointing, but keep in mind that you are probably not alone in being told this. No need to take it personally. What makes you different from everyone else is how you deal or cope with the disappointment. It's just business.

THINGS THAT GIVE ME A BOOST . . . Make a list of ten things that give you a jump start, and use all of them.

1. _____

2. _____

3. _____

4. _____

5. _____

6. _____

7. _____

8. _____

9. _____

10. _____

A primary reason for not hiring someone who is overqualified is because that company views you as someone who will likely move on quickly to a better job. Companies would rather invest time and money in an employee for a long-term business than go through the rehiring and training process six months later. By not hiring you, they're only doing what they believe is best for their company. Likewise, you don't want to make a commitment to a job you know you have no intention of keeping for the future. Although disappointing, it is the best situation for you both.

This shouldn't prohibit you from seeking employment where you have obvious skills to perform. If you've been at the top of your field, it will be that much harder to find an equal or similar job, especially for older people competing with a younger workforce. It's time to make the best of a new situation—keep in mind, your situation isn't better or worse, it's just different. This is also an opportunity to get out of your com-

How to Avoid Being Overqualified

- Tailor your résumé. Customize it to meet the specific needs of the hiring employer. Try to weed out extra qualifications that may instantly disqualify you.

- Keep the cover letter short and simple. The cover letter serves only as your introduction to the company. Hit your selling points briefly and do not repeat your résumé—let it speak for itself.

- Communicate the idea that there is value and honor in every job. During the interview, if asked about salary, bear in mind there is a difference between what a job is worth and what you may be worth. You may want to openly communicate that you are available to work for less than you are worth and most importantly, why. You may also want to consider telling the hiring employer why you are no more likely to move to another job than anyone else applying for the same position.

fort zone and find something new, exciting, or completely different. Many people view accepting a position that they are overqualified for as taking a step back on the career ladder. Get out of your ego! As long as you keep that belief system, you may be miserable in a job that might provide much needed income or a starting point for higher career development than your previous track. You have been given an opportunity. Cherish it. Make the most of the time while you have it. Take the chance to meet people you wouldn't normally meet.

BE STILL

Having read chapter after chapter of things to keep you busy for days, weeks, months, and even years, you may be surprised at the following suggestion: Do nothing. Be still. Let your spirit be still and it will guide you. The tendency when reacting to any emergency or significant life change is to slip into a permanent crisis-management mode. We make the shift from putting all our energy for our previous employment into finding our next one. Slow down, there is no need to rush. Quiet your mind to better connect to your spirit or the divine.

Be calm. Let tranquility wash over you. Feel the moment of each breath. Experience each heartbeat. Find places to be at peace—in the mountains; in a park; by a stream; in a meadow or field; in a quiet room in the house, patio, or garden. We are at our best during moments of peace and quiet. Take time to look within yourself, to do self-discovery work, to determine what and where you want to go. Introspection can be a powerful tool in making career and life decisions, in finding new directions, or in rededicating your life purposes. Support the faith in your life that the opportunities will come. Know that all is well and will be well.

A new job, a different career, a new place to live, and unique opportunities may be waiting right in front of you. If you are too busy being busy and so proactive with your life, you may not be listening to the still, small voices of inspiration and wise counsel. Surprisingly, there are many people who say the best work they did to find a job was to do nothing. They stopped reading classifieds, networking, or sending out résumés. They supported their patience enough to allow opportunities to present themselves. Instead of hurrying to a new crossroad, let the path choose or find you.

CHAPTER 8

END THE DAY AT 5 P.M.

Many people spend 24/7 worrying about the issues associated with being unemployed. But being unemployed is a job unto itself, and like a job, when the whistle blows at 5 p.m., your day needs to end so that you may tend to the rest of your life. On the best of days we need to take breaks, but during turbulent times you'll need to give yourself a break even more—you don't have to worry about your job status all the time. Right now, your job is to find employment; but just like a regular job, if you don't check out at 5 p.m., you'll diminish your value and impair your ability to perform the next day. Since most businesses close at 5 p.m., there isn't much job-hunting you can do until the next morning. So there's no reason to continue worrying about it tonight.

Some of us have the habit of not ending the day at a reasonable time to give attention to other aspects of our lives. If so, you have been robbing yourself of much enjoyment and a wealth of other opportunities that are available. If you continue to struggle with ending your day earlier, try experimenting for a short time, and see if your life and overall happiness improves. If this short experiment is still not working, you may need a little help. Ask for some "supervision" from a family member or friend. Ask them to open your door at 5 p.m., and flood the room with your kids or dog announcing the end of the day. If nobody is home, ask them to call you and say, "Are you having fun yet?" Or, "I'm coming by and you be better be up to something fun by the time I get there or else."

Give yourself permission to do what you would typically do at the end of the day. Enjoy dinner at home with your family or friends. Read a book, watch your favorite television program—whatever it takes. Just be sure to take yourself off the clock.

Adopt a New Mantra: T.G.I. Thursday

When you're working full time, Friday night can't come soon enough. For most people, when Friday does finally come, it's cause to honor the traditional "Thank Goodness It's Friday!" celebration. However, when you're unemployed and expending energy on searching for a job, get used to saying a new weekend mantra: "Thank Goodness It's Thursday!" Your weekend is now in sight a day earlier, and the light at the end of the tunnel isn't necessarily a train about to run you over. Congratulations, your weekend begins here.

For most people, job searching uses a lot of physical and emotional energy. You only have so much energy in a given week, and job hunting expends your current allowance of energy and depletes your reserves that much faster. Spending four full days sending out résumés and interviewing is equivalent to working a typical 9-to-5, five-day-a-week job. There is no shame or guilt in admitting when you're done for the week. But, when you're done, and your tank is dry and you know it, you need to stop and walk away—just like a normal Friday when you were employed. If you work any more, you're engaging in deficit spending of your emotional energy account by using more energy than you're creating.

Working or not, we all create, preserve, and expend our energy reserves. Some people may find they can continue to function at the same level they did while employed, working feverishly five, six, even seven days a week. These are the lucky few. While job searching, if you find yourself not being able to do much come Friday morning, don't worry about it. Millions of people across the country are feeling the same way during their employment search. The best you can do is step back from the job-hunting process and begin to recharge your batteries by enjoying your Friday!

TAKE SOME TIME OFF

Most people who are unemployed don't give themselves permission to take any extended time off from job hunting. Make this a priority; you need the time off. Just like when you're working full time, you need time off to clear your head and get away from it all. Start by taking an afternoon or a day off and schedule your weekends to be work-free just like everybody else. It's okay to go play, to hang out with your friends, or be with your family. Do what you would normally do, minus the major expenses.

Sometimes, clearing your head, relaxing, and revitalizing your energy can be as positive and productive as spending all day looking for work. During the week, take time to walk in the park, make necessary home repairs, or go to a movie. It's okay, you're not being a bum. Take a vacation—yes, a vacation. Maybe not right away, as you do have a lot of work to do, but just as you need a vacation while employed, you need a vacation from your job of being unemployed. There are some wonderful ways to vacation inexpensively. You don't have to jet off to Europe or take expensive cruises. Take a stay-at-home vacation. Or, if you want to get away, vacation inexpensively:

- Go camping instead of paying for pricey hotel rooms.
- Stay with friends or family out of town.
- Take day trips to nearby areas without spending the night or buying expensive meals.
- Use the frequent-flyer miles you've been saving.
- Research and travel to hotels during their inexpensive days of the week.
- Rent a condo at a great location with a group of friends.
- Visit countries that cost much less to travel.

- Travel during off-season or shoulder seasons (trips that normally cost thousands could be in the hundreds).

- Consider staying at a youth hostel for adults and families.

- Search Web sites for last-minute deals for airfare, hotels, car rentals, and cruises.

- Check out air courier or consolidator travel for traveling privileges.

- Research Lonely Planet Guides, Fodor's, or travel club information for inexpensive travel tips.

We sometimes think that taking time off means that we are being irresponsible and neglecting our hunt for employment. But by getting away, be it a weekend adventure or an overnight trip to the country, you'll find you are more energized to continue your job-search activities.

SEEK OUT FREE ACTIVITIES

Under any circumstances, fun and self-nurturing activities should be part of daily life. Now you'll need to have fun more than ever. It's just like needing blood during surgery—pump it in! It's surprising how many activities are available for free:

- Find out about your public library's activities.

- Write in a journal.
- Go for a walk.

- Play with your pet.
- Listen to music.

- Ride a bike.
- Go window-shopping.

- Attend free lectures or workshops.
- Enjoy public nature preserves.

- Go to court and watch a trial.

- Attend community concerts at churches or parks.

- Browse the farmers' markets, or visit harvest and cultural festivals.

- Participate in community gardening projects.
- Take a city walking tour and see the various places of interest in your own community.
- Sit in on legislative sessions or city council meetings.
- Visit beach communities or city parks that often have volleyball or tennis courts set up along with swing sets and play areas for children.
- Watch your favorite weekly TV programs—comedy, drama, adventure, travel, nature and sports, or other shows on home improvement, gardening, cooking, or interior design. Keep in mind that if your leisure activity includes TV and you watch too much, you run the risk of losing precious energy. Like anything, moderation is the key.
- Find a new place to walk, in-line skate, or jog.
- Attend book readings at local bookstores and libraries.
- Get rid of the stale bread in the fridge by feeding ducks at the local pond, lake, or river.
- Call your local junior college or university and find out about public events, lectures, and activities being offered to the students.
- Call the local tourist office for a list of information on what activities the tourists are doing for free.

You'll be surprised at what your city has to offer, and how much of it is free. Use this as a chance to discover the many wonderful opportunities waiting for you right in your own community. Now is a great time to take advantage of them—especially since they're free.

HAVE FUN ON A DIME

What is the goal of going out for dinner or the movies? Time to be with your friends and having fun? To be entertained? To get away from it all? To avoid cooking? Just because you're unemployed doesn't mean you have to give up these activities. In fact—play! Just play within your budget. Here are great time-spenders—without being budget-busters:

- Go to museums, art galleries, and bargain movies.
- Rent videos or host potluck meals with friends.
- Pursue your artistic interests at the local community center; attend a class on painting, pencil sketching, sculpting, or pottery.
- Make a mix of your favorite songs.
- Most communities offer a free local paper that lists activities and events in the city. This can be everything from which clubs have what bands playing to a variety of festivals and events. These are usually found at coffee shops or convenience stores. The weekend section in the local newspaper is also a good source to find out what events are going on in your town that range from free to expensive.
- Go to outdoor and camping shows.
- See home improvement demonstrations.
- Take local botanical garden tours.   • Visit art festivals.
- Fly a kite on a windy day.   • Go fishing.
- Drive around historical neighborhoods and sightsee. Better yet, take a walking historical home tour in your area.
- Have coffee at a local outdoor café and read the newspaper.
- Visit your corner coffeehouse for a poetry reading or slam.
- Burn incense, light candles, or enjoy aromatherapy.
- Seek out community carnivals or barbecues.
- Visit a nearby state or national park, or find access to the nearest national forest.

- Pack a picnic and spend a day outdoors.

- If you live near a large body of water or a coastal area, take a ferry ride and enjoy the serenity.

- Take yourself or your family to the local zoo.

- If you have kids, invest in an annual, unlimited access pass to the local amusement or water park.

When you are unemployed, spending a dollar can feel like spending a hundred dollars and even an inexpensive activity can feel very expensive. In times of greatest need, try to have a little faith that your money will last, and value yourself by spending a little to make yourself feel like a million bucks.

INDULGE IN RETAIL THERAPY

After reading all the previous penny-pinching chapters, you may be surprised that retail therapy is suggested in times of financial stress. Done wisely, it can be a great stress-buster or diversion. And it's almost always done after a long, hard day. But sometimes, when the going gets tough, the tough need to go shopping!

Shopping makes us feel better when we're having a bad day. Sometimes we experience a heightened emotional experience that improves our mood when we buy something. Why not take advantage of that great feeling while buying something for almost nothing? While unemployed, people often learn how inexpensive life really can be. It can be a very creative and empowering process to cut costs and get by financially in a more efficient manner. Ask yourself this: Why pay retail when I can buy wholesale? Where do the expensive retailers buy their merchandise, anyway? There's a whole world of bargain living out there:

- Thrift stores: These stores are perfect for the bargain hunter.

- Dollar shops: These carry items that can be handy around the house, such as food, soaps, hangers, and dish cloths.

Ten Survival Tips for the Unemployed Shopper

1. Only take a small amount of cash with you and leave credit cards at home. This will help to avoid impulse spending.

2. Before purchasing anything, ask yourself, "Do I really need this? Is this something I can live without?"

3. Keep track of receipts. When you get home, review what purchases you made and repeat step 2 above.

4. Avoid expensive department stores and boutiques.

5. Never buy anything at full price.

6. Be careful of pushy salespeople. They're not the one without a job, so remember your budget when they tell you something looks wonderful on you.

7. Don't look at tempting displays strategically placed near cash wraps and escalators.

8. If you have children, it will be easier to leave them at home with a sitter. It may be difficult to avoid buying more, especially if your child is pleading, "Can I have this?" or "I want that."

9. If shopping for the holidays, make a list of people for whom to shop and keep a checklist next to each name of what you're buying. This will help you to stay focused on exactly what you're looking for.

10. Be careful of bulk shopping and buying too many items on sale. You may be coughing up money for items you may not use. For now, it's more practical for you to only buy what you need.

- Consignment shops: These are more upscale-looking shops that carry designer labels. Owners and donators split profits when merchandise is sold. If your closet is full of trendy clothes you no longer wear, consider taking your stuff here for some extra cash.

- Flea markets: Find everything from furniture to dishes to clothing at these inexpensive markets.

- Garage and yard sales: You can find clothes, furniture, sporting equipment, and toys at prices you can negotiate.

- Discount wholesale retailers: This is name-brand bargain shopping for the family. Usually imperfect merchandise for women, men, and children are for sale.

- Upscale resale shops: These boutiques are known for pampering their shoppers. Get away with paying a third of what you would normally pay if these outfits were found at a department store.

- Vintage stores: Looking for some faded jeans that don't cost a bundle? While digging through one of these stores, you're sure to find some pop culture keepsakes.

Have fun by heading for the mall, even if you don't purchase a thing! Spending an hour, an afternoon, or an entire Saturday bargain hunting or window-shopping can be a great way to release stress and step away from your worries for a while. Plus, shopping is something that can be done alone, in tandem, or in packs. It's a great socializing process, but bear in mind that you must be budget-wise and dollar-smart. When it's all said and done, be sure to show off your $45 shirt that you got for five bucks!

Take Care: Monday Ahead!

It's Sunday night already. After enjoying a nice, relaxing weekend away from the pressures and challenges of job searching and worrying over bills, Sunday night can be the worst night of the week. Sunday brings feelings of dread that "Black Monday II: The Sequel" will be lurking with the morning paper on the doorstep.

Most everyone dislikes Monday. How many cartoons, songs, or posters deal with the drudgery of facing Monday morning? When you're unemployed, Monday is that much worse. Your weekend time off is like a weekly cease-fire from all the minutiae and details of looking for work. It is a chance to recharge your batteries and re-create yourself. Undoubtedly, with all the

Do You Have Anticipatory Anxiety?

- Are you nervous before beginning a challenging activity?

- Do you ruminate on conversations you may engage in?

- Are you anxious when thinking about difficult tasks?

- Do you have mood swings when anticipating certain activities?

- Do you have a loss of appetite before you attend to difficult tasks?

turmoil of finding new employment lingering, waiting, and creeping up on you on Sunday, facing Monday is tough. Often, it's the anticipation of Monday's arrival that makes it worse.

Anticipatory anxiety is a common experience for millions of people. It is anxiety or stress associated with participating in future activities such as a job interview or unpleasant tasks. In essence, it is caused by fearful expectations. In general, anxiety is a normal response to threatening situations and serves as a natural coping mechanism to survival. It keeps us alert to possible danger, and can be used as energy to motivate us to action and change. Unfortunately, we can get too much of a good thing. It may be difficult to motivate yourself for Monday morning, fighting feelings of angst for the long week ahead, and bracing to continue your search for full-time employment without going crazy in the process.

When the anxiety demons loom late on Sunday night, you'll need to rely on your favorite anxiety-busters to see you through Sunday's weaning hours. We've talked about many of those listed below, but we've also included a few extras:

- Go for a walk.

- Talk with friends or family.

- Take a hot bath.

- Write in your journal.

- Enjoy music.

- Practice deep breathing.

- Visualize yourself in a beautiful place.

- Think of a time or moment when you have faced adversity with success or had a great learning experience.

- Be confident in facing your fears.

- Close your eyes and visualize yourself in a beautiful or comfortable setting.

- Transform or replace negative thoughts into positive thoughts about the future and excitement for pending successes.

- Adopt positive affirmations to boost your self-confidence and restore your sense of balance.

You can't fight your dragons before they arrive; Monday will come soon enough. Until then, enjoy the rest of your weekend, have fun, and live in the present—not in the future. This way, you'll have your batteries fully loaded and ready to begin the new week when it actually arrives.

DIGESTING IT ALL

Life is often filled with obstacles and uncertainty. But failure in life is only when we view our hardships as stumbling blocks rather than stepping-stones toward new experiences and personal growth. Your greatest challenges can become your greatest gifts. There are a lot of people who find themselves stranded in difficult situations, mistakes, or failures, and never move beyond them, while other people use these opportunities for personal growth and transformation and eventually appreciate the challenges they have overcome. If you're unhappy, work to find joy, move forward, and improve yourself and the life you're living.

Even though it may not seem like it at this moment, there are many things to be excited about in your life. If you've read this book and taken some of these suggestions, you already have a lot more going for you than you realize. Take care of yourself, have some fun, and follow the advice in this book to help with your emotional well-being. You'll be the better for it. We can promise you that tomorrow, the sun will rise, you'll wake up, and a new day will begin.

REFERENCES

American Academy of Sleep Medicine, n.d. http://www.aasmnet.org (September 4, 2003).

Bureau of Labor Statistics, n.d. http://www.bls.gov (August 20, 2003).

Dr. Tim Evans, Rotary Club speech for CHOICE (Center for Humanitarian Outreach and Cultural Exchange), September 2000.

Food and Agriculture Organization of the United Nations, n.d. http://www.fao.org (July 11, 2002).

"How Laughter Works," n.d. http://www.people.howstuffworks.com/laughter.htm (August 21, 2003).

Jampolsky, Jerry, and Diane V. Cirincione. Forgiveness Works, n.d. http://www.forgivenessworks.org (September 5, 2003).

Monster.com, n.d. http://www.monster.com (September 4, 2003).

Monterey Preventive Medical Clinic, n.d. http://www.wellnessmd.com (September 4, 2003).

National Sleep Foundation, n.d. http://www.sleepfoundation.org (September 4, 2003).

Center for Online and Internet Addiction, n.d. http://www.netaddiction.com (September 3, 2003).

National Vital Statistics Report, Vol. 49, No. 12, March 2002.

"As Economy Sours, Divorce Rates Rise." The New York Times. June 17, 2001.

UNICEF, n.d. http://www.unicef.org (July 11, 2002).

United States National Agricultural Library, n.d. http://www.nal.usda.gov (August 19, 2003).

United States Surgeon General, n.d. http://www.surgeongeneral.gov (June 25, 2003).

"Obese Americans Get a Tax Break." USA Today Information Network. April 3, 2002.

Utah Department of Workforce Services, n.d. http://www.jobs.utah.gov (June 25, 2003).

World Health Organization, n.d. http://www.who.int (July 11, 2002).

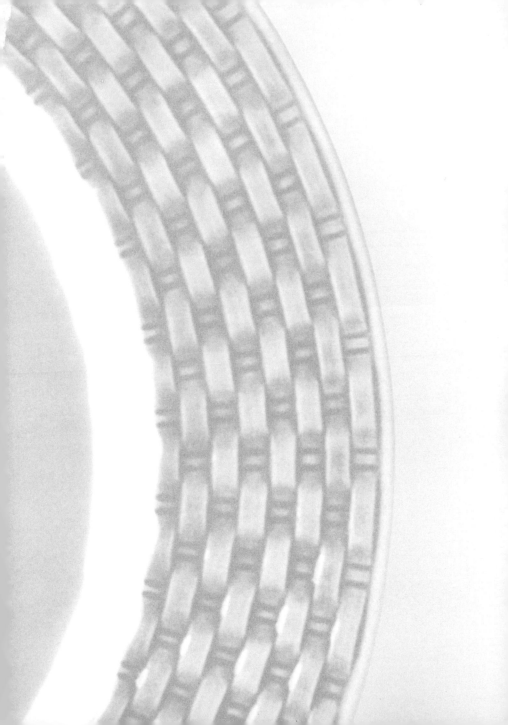